D0609175

H. E. Bates

Twayne's English Authors Series

Kinley E. Roby, Editor
Northeastern University

TEAS 358

H. E. Bates
(1905 – 1974)
Photograph courtesy of Michael Joseph, Ltd., London

H. E. Bates

By Dennis Vannatta

University of Arkansas at Little Rock

Twayne Publishers · Boston

H. E. Bates

Dennis Vannatta

Copyright © 1983 by G. K. Hall & Company
All Rights Reserved
Published by Twayne Publishers
A Division of G. K. Hall & Company
70 Lincoln Street
Boston, Massachusetts 02111

Book Production by John Amburg
Book Design by Barbara Anderson

Printed on permanent/durable acid-free
paper and bound in the United States of
America.

Library of Congress Cataloging in Publication Data

Vannatta, Dennis P.
H.E. Bates.

(Twayne's English authors series;
TEAS 358)
Bibliography: p. 138
Includes index.
1. Bates, H. E. (Herbert Ernest),
1905 – 1974—
Criticism and interpretation.
I. Title. II. Series.
PR6003.A965Z93   1983   823'.912   82-21329
ISBN 0-8057-6844-0

Contents

About the Author

Dennis Vannatta received the Bachelor of Science in Education degree from Central Missouri State College (1968) and the Master of Arts (1972) and Doctor of Philosophy (1978) degrees from the University of Missouri—Columbia, where he concentrated in twentieth-century fiction. He has published one book—*Nathanael West: An Annotated Bibliography of the Scholarship and Works* (Garland, 1976)—and articles (published or forthcoming) on William Gass, V. S. Pritchett, Alain Robbe-Grillet, Tim O'Brien, James Dickey, and Max Apple. He presently teaches contemporary literature, the short story, and writing courses at the University of Arkansas at Little Rock, where he is an associate professor.

Preface

Herbert Ernest (H. E.) Bates (1905 – 1974) published his first novel, *The Two Sisters*, in 1926 at the age of twenty, and his subsequent career as a novelist, short-story writer, essayist, and sometime poet and dramatist spanned almost a half-century. As a writer of short fiction he has been compared favorably to Chekhov, Katherine Mansfield, and D. H. Lawrence by fellow writers and critics. His novels were less well received critically; but *The Two Sisters* was still in print as late as 1970, and many of his post – World War II novels, especially the Pop Larkin series, achieved wide popularity in England. In all, Bates published twenty-three novels, nineteen collections of short stories (plus a dozen selected editions), over twenty novellas, two plays, a few "occasional" poems, a critical history of the short story, scores of essays and monographs on natural history and personal reminiscences, plus a three-volume autobiography. The consistent high quality of his work over all or part of six decades makes Bates the personification of literary professionalism.

Despite the quantity and quality of Bates's work, his name is hardly well known among American readers. More puzzling, given the virtual explosion of literary scholarship over the last two decades, is the fact that scholars have for the most part ignored Bates's work. To my knowledge only one dissertation has been written on Bates and only one article published. Critical comment has been largely restricted to a mass of reviews and notices, brief mentions in literary surveys, and the usual summaries in reference works. The aim of this study, then, is to offer an introduction to a neglected writer.

I have chosen to restrict my comments almost exclusively to Bates's fiction since there his literary strengths, past popularity, and future reputation obviously lie. Bates's talents as a poet were minimal, by his own admission, and his involvement in drama was too brief and undistinguished to be of consequence. Even eliminating these, it would be infeasible to attempt an in-depth analysis of each of the forty-odd volumes of fiction which Bates published in his career. I have, rather, attempted an overview of Bates's thematic and stylistic development, pausing for a closer examination of representative works.

The first chapter of this study is biographical in nature, dealing with Bates's early years. Although he was not an autobiographical writer to the extent that Hemingway and Joyce often were, Bates's rearing and experiences in the Midland villages of his youth had an impact on his work from first to last. Throughout the subsequent chapters I have tried to draw upon the literary, historical, and social currents that had a major influence on Bates's life and writing.

Many persons were helpful to me in one way or another during my work on this study. Certainly, the interlibrary loan personnel at the University of Missouri—Columbia and the University of Arkansas at Little Rock made a vast amount of material readily available, and I gratefully acknowledge their assistance. And, as always, I want to thank my wife and daughter for providing the human context without which intellectual pursuits are irrelevant.

I also want to thank Professor Kinley E. Roby for his very perceptive and helpful suggestions for editing and revising the manuscript of this work. Finally, I want especially to thank William Peden, Professor Emeritus at the University of Missouri—Columbia, who introduced me to the pleasures of H. E. Bates's fiction and first encouraged me to do this study, and to whom this book is dedicated.

Dennis Vannatta

University of Arkansas at Little Rock

Acknowledgments

I gratefully acknowledge permission from Evensford Productions, the estate of H. E. Bates and Laurence Pollinger Limited to quote from the following works by H. E. Bates: *The Two Sisters, Day's End and Other Stories, Seven Tales and Alexander, Catherine Foster, The Black Boxer, The Woman Who Had Imagination and Other Stories, Cut and Come Again, Something Short and Sweet, The Fallow Land, The Poacher, A House of Women, Spella Ho, My Uncle Silas, The Beauty of the Dead and Other Stories, Fair Stood the Wind for France, The Cruise of the Breadwinner, The Purple Plain, The Jacaranda Tree, Dear Life, Colonel Julian and Other Stories, The Daffodil Sky, Sugar for the Horse, The Watercress Girl and Other Stories, The Wedding Party, Love for Lydia, The Feast of July, A Little of What You Fancy, The Distant Horns of Summer, The Grapes of Paradise, The Golden Oriole, The Four Beauties, The Triple Echo, The Modern Short Story,* "Introduction" to *Six Stories,* "Thomas Hardy and Joseph Conrad" in *The English Novel: A Survey of the Novel by Twenty Contemporary Novelists.*

I gratefully acknowledge the permission of the University of Missouri Press to quote from the following works:

Reprinted from *The Vanished World: An Autobiography* by H. E. Bates, by permission of the University of Missouri Press. Copyright 1969 by Evensford Productions Ltd.; United States edition published by the University of Missouri Press.

Reprinted from *The Blossoming World: An Autobiography* by H. E. Bates, by permission of the University of Missouri Press. Copyright 1971 by Evensford Productions Ltd.; United States edition published by the University of Missouri Press.

Reprinted from *The World in Ripeness: An Autobiography* by H. E. Bates, by permission of the University of Missouri Press. Copyright 1972 by Evensford Productions Ltd.; United States edition published by the University of Missouri Press, 1972.

Chronology

1905   Herbert Ernest Bates born in Rushden, Northamptonshire, 16 May.

1916   Granted free tuition and railway fares to the grammar school at Kettering.

1921   Turns down opportunity to go to Cambridge, leaves school for good.

1922   Works as junior reporter for the *Northampton Chronicle*; begins first novel (never published) while working as warehouseman.

1926   *The Last Bread* (Labour Publishing Company), a play: first published book; *The Two Sisters* (Jonathan Cape): first published novel.

1927   Tours Europe with Rhys Davies and others.

1928   *Day's End and Other Stories*.

1929   *Catherine Foster*; *Seven Tales and Alexander*.

1931   Marries Marjorie Helen Cox; *Charlotte's Row*.

1932   Begins to write "Country Life" column for the *Spectator*; daughter Anne Catharine born; *The Black Boxer*; *The Fallow Land*.

1933   Daughter Judith born.

1935   *Cut and Come Again: Fourteen Stories*; *The Poacher*.

1936   *A House of Women*.

1937   Son Richard Lucas born; *Something Short and Sweet: Stories*.

1938   *Spella Ho*; goes to America to edit *Spella Ho* for the *Atlantic Monthly*.

1939   *The Flying Goat*; *My Uncle Silas: Stories*.

1940   Son Jonathan born; *The Beauty of the Dead and Other Stories*.

1941   Becomes literary editor for the *Spectator*; commissioned in the Air Ministry as a short-story writer.

1942   *The Greatest People in the World and Other Stories* (as Flying Officer "X").

1943   *How Sleep the Brave and Other Stories* (as Flying Officer "X"); changes publishers, from Jonathan Cape to Michael Joseph; takes on Laurence Pollinger as agent.

Chapter One
Bates's Early Years

A Northamptonshire Lad

Surely the air was filled with birdsong and flowers splashed the English Midland meadows with color on that May day (the sixteenth, 1905) when Herbert Ernest Bates was born. Only such a day could appropriately herald the birth of a writer whose work is memorable for its striking descriptions of nature. Dog-roses, meadowsweet, and willow-herb graced the countryside only a few minutes' walk from Rushden, Northamptonshire, Bates's birthplace; and his earliest memories are suffused with a love of the natural world: "Stickle-backs were in the brook, cuckoos called from the elms, yellowhammers swooned away long summer afternoons in lanes shimmering with heat and virtually undefiled by the motor-car, and consequently all was right with the world."[1]

But all was not right with young Bates's world; Rushden itself was a "palpably ugly mess of that mixture of blue slate, factory, chapel and that harsh Midland red brick which equally oppresses heart, soul, and eye" (*Vanished World*, 33). The contrasting worlds of bucolic splendor and urban blight prefigures the war of opposites which marks Bates's fiction from first to last: the struggle matching the desire for freedom of body and spirit against such forces of inhibition as religion, poverty, false morality, and authority figures.

The Rushden of Bates's youth was one of those small English communities which transformed from a country village to a factory town during the Industrial Revolution. The shoemaking industry was the economic heart of Rushden; and although we might like to think of Bates, the prose-singer of nature, as being descended from yeoman farm stock, the truth is that his immediate ancestors were far more intimate with the tongue of a boot than the tongue of a hay-wagon. Both of his grandfathers were shoemakers; his father owned his own boot and shoemaking business; and his mother began tying knots for two shillings a week at the age of ten. Indeed, the song of the meadowlark may have been often in Bates's ears as a lad, but the sixty-year-old laments in his autobiography that if he ever succumbs to a sickness of the lungs, "it may

well be because the distant pungent odours of leather and shoemakers'
shops still linger tenaciously within me" (*Vanished World,* 7).
Even within the world of the shoemakers we sense the fusion of the
negative and the positive which Bates felt to be so essential to the writer
of fiction. In his heart the cobbler was a hardy, independent craftsman,
devoted to his trade but no more so than to the pleasures of good drink
and fellowship, the joys of the field, forest, and stream out of which only
a few generations past he had come to settle in the towns. Bates recalls
that in the golden years of the craft

There were no forty hour weeks, no clocking in. Forever independent, shoemakers were ever a law unto themselves, mostly getting rousing drunk on
Saturdays and Sundays, never by long tradition working on Mondays. Either
out of duty to their patron St. Crispin or in pursuit of a cure for mountainous
hangovers, they sought solace in the surrounding countryside, rabbiting,
coursing, mushrooming, following hounds, walking or riding miles by devious
routes to secret hide-outs where bare-fisted bruisers bloodily battered themselves to pulp before crowds of gentry and poor alike. (*Vanished World,* 13 – 14)

Unfortunately, by the time of Bates's youth those golden years largely
were finished. The cobbler's bench gave way to the factory, and the
timetable became king. Thus, instead of being lord of his craft, the
shoemaker became a slave to it. Juxtaposed to his memories of laughter
amid fields and forests are scenes of dye-blackened men dashing madly
through the streets to be on time for the morning shift. Bates went to the
factories, too, bringing his father's tea, and the vision is hardly joyous: "I
used to go to this dark, ugly, dreary, noisome, thunderous bedlam of
industry with a sense of dread: not dread, I think, of its sheer drabness,
its stench of leather and gaslight or its racket of presses and whining
scream of machines, but a terrible dread at the half-conscious notion that
one day I too might have to work in it" (*Vanished World,* 36).
Bates never did have to work in the factories, largely, perhaps,
because of his father's resolve against such a future for his son. Still, it is
little wonder that in the fiction of the mature Bates the sprawl of
industrial society will always be portrayed with such loathing, that
stories with industrial settings will consistently be somber in tone,
pessimistic in spirit. Little wonder that the elder Bates will survey the
manufactured "marvels" of the contemporary age and moan, "The world
of television, jets and space craft dazzles our generation with new if
sometimes near useless wonders, but for myself I would cheerfully
exchange it for . . . the smell of wood-smoke, the scent of blue-bells,

cowslips, primrose, and the Maiden's Blush, the Turk's Cap Lily, and the voices of nightingales" (*Vanished World*, 61).

The destruction of natural beauty by industrial blight would indeed disturb Bates throughout his life, but the resulting blight on the human spirit represents by far the greater evil for Bates the man and writer. Ironically, Bates's father—so insistent on saving his son from the tyranny of the timetable and factory whistle—himself never escaped. The deeper irony lies in the fact that his father came to represent an inhibiting force at least as loathsome to his son as the factories: organized religion.

The Fraud of Religion

If the secular world of Rushden hastened to the shriek of the factory whistle, the sectarian world answered the call of the church bell—Low Church in this case. Perhaps Bates's father's rigid Methodism was an extreme reaction to his own father's capricious morality; Bates's grandfather "neglected" to marry his grandmother, then sailed for Australia in later years in search of greener pastures. Bates would have preferred Australia to chapel on Sundays, which came to seem little more than a day of imprisonment: "I am unfamiliar with what contemporary Methodism now produces in the way of its more dedicated adherents, but fifty years ago it was still dominated by stern and tyrannical believers who upheld the piety of silence, were convinced that even whispering among boys was a sin and had no compunction about boxing the ears of the recalcitrant with bible or hymn book as a penalty for the minutest misdemeanor" (*Vanished World*, 62−63). Bates's spiritual break from his father became irrevocable when he reached the conclusion that organized religion was "a boney bore, a monstrous fraud, a body of hypocrisy with no drop of living blood in all its veins, no purpose in all its works" (*Vanished World*, 178).

The result in Bates's fiction of his disenchantment with Methodism is clear: organized religion becomes an object of scorn, its ministers clowns and charlatans. The philosophical implications of Bates's apostasy are more far-reaching. Bates will treat morality itself as little more than an artificial construct having no higher purpose than to enslave the spirit. At the extreme, in "Thomas Hardy and Joseph Conrad," an essay in which Bates attacks Hardy's moral provincialism, he concludes that "morality, as a fixed entity, does not really exist, that it is nothing but a fashion. . . . Morality is virtually a fraud, since there is really no stabilized coinage of morality at all but only the elemental currency of human action and re-action, human conduct and its consequences."[2] As we shall see, for the characters in Bates's created world the only immoral state will be unhappiness and the only immoral action that which causes unhappiness.

Although his father personifies the enervating religion that Bates so despised, and although in his fiction father-figures will consistently be portrayed as oppressive, parsimonious, even brutal, it would be a distortion to claim that in his autobiography Bates ever poses his father as a villian. His father is more victim than victimizer. A shoemaker early in life, an independent shop-owner later, the elder Bates never escaped the world of leather and dye from which he vowed to save his son. And although Bates might have chafed under his father's religious reins, we detect a son's pride in a father whose home exuded "an atmosphere of intense respectability" (*Vanished World*, 29) and whose industry kept his family in that class of Midlanders who are "a notch above a tapper" (*Vanished World*, 44).

The hero of Bates's early life was not his father, however, but George William Lucas, his maternal grandfather. At an age when a change in profession would surely be traumatic, Lucas left the shoemaking business and bought a small farm. The land was wickedly poor, and the chance for material success was almost nil, but to Bates the farm was a joy. It was with Lucas that Bates went haying and fruit picking, and it was to this rather irascible and enigmatic free spirit that Bates paid the ultimate compliment: "His true God, like mine, was really nature."[3]

The temptation is great to see the two major formative influences in Bates's life, his father and grandfather, as archetypal opposites. The one had nature for his god and returned to the land from the city; the other remained in the factory town and prayed to a more civilized, stricter god. Again and again in his autobiography we see Bates being pulled between these opposing angels, and Bates was aware of the resultant dichotomy in his personality: "There has always been in my character this strong pull of conscience on one side and disposition to flout authority on the other" (*Vanished World*, 122–23).

The Schoolhouse Prison

With his love of the freedom of fields and woods established at an early age and his "disposition to flout authority" at least inchoate, it is hardly surprising that young Bates greeted the prospect of being shut away in a schoolhouse less than enthusiastically. Indeed, Bates recalls that he "viewed the prospect of attending it with as much dread as going to prison . . ." (*Vanished World*, 42). Despite those early fears, young Bates (he was three or four when he first went to the elementary school in Rushden) was a superior student. In fact, by the time he was seven he was moved to a special desk apart from the other students and given advanced work.

The apogee and nadir of Bates's scholarly career occurred simultaneously, in 1916, on the day that he was selected, along with a half-dozen of his fellow students, to take the scholarship examination for the public school at Wellingborough. Bates was the only one to fail. Although eventually he was granted a "free place"—free tuition and railway fares—at the grammar school at Kettering, his disappointment was deep and lasting. From this time on Bates's educational career was little more than a waste of disillusionment, school little more than a secular Methodism: a place of imprisonment ruled for the most part by incompetents, rigid dogmatists, even sadists. The Bates of early adolescence was a good athlete but an apathetic student, given to pranks and daydreams and indifferent to almost all subjects, including literature. His one interest was art, and the crowning achievements resulting from that interest found their way not to the Louvre or the Prado, but to his mother's bedroom wall: "an extraordinary and inimitable pair of pictures, since they are beyond all doubt the two worst pictures ever painted by man" (*Vanished World*, 101).

How, we might ask, from such apparently infertile grounds did there spring the author of hundreds of short stories, two-dozen novels, two plays, a volume of literary criticism, and scores of books and essays ranging from natural history to biography to a three-volume autobiography? Fortunately for Bates and for the literary world, his father, unimaginative in many ways, had a thorough respect for education in general and a devotion to reading of all sorts. Bates, listless in school, avidly devoured the contents of his father's library, which contained in bound volumes such periodicals as the *Strand*, the *Harmsworth*, and the *Windsor*, plus novels by an assortment of authors. Of the authors encountered by Bates—Conan Doyle, Kipling, Barrie, William le Queux, E. Phillips Oppenheim, Edgar Wallace, and so forth—some are still read while others have been relegated to literary oblivion; but from all of them Bates learned a lesson that would become the *idée fixe* of his writing career:

. . . I unconsciously assimilated something of their methods—by which I mean the way all of them had no time for wasting words but had to make their points economically and incisively, rejecting all highly descriptive padding; an assimilation which, though unconscious at the time, as I say, was later to emerge as a guiding principle when I myself began to handle the short story. Even now I can remember expressing sharp impatience if a story went on too long, an impatience that has probably led to my disposition to stop stories short, leaving the reader in a state of speculative suspense and wondering guess-work, rather than take him on to a well-ordered and boring end. (*Vanished World*, 45−46)

Perhaps the bright spot of an otherwise nondescript educational career came when Bates was fourteen. His teacher had assigned the class to write an essay on Shakespeare. For the first time Bates felt the thrill of literary creation, and thereafter he would find himself immersed more and more in writing. Bates's formal education came to an end in 1921. That year he won "honors" on an examination for the Joint Oxford and Cambridge University Certificate but turned down an opportunity to attend Cambridge, due to the financial stress such a decision would have placed on his family. It was a decision he never regretted.

The Odd-Job Man

No longer confined to school, Bates spent his days roaming the fields and writing bad poetry. In 1922 he accepted a job as a junior reporter on the *Northampton Chronicle*, seemingly an ideal training ground for a budding young writer. Unfortunately, Bates found his duties—visiting the coroner's office and police station and posting racing results—boring and depressing. He resigned after two months.

Later that year, Bates found a job as a warehouseman: a fortuitous event, for his new occupation earned him the few shillings a week that he desperately needed but still allowed him time to write. And write he did: poems, short stories, and, at the age of seventeen, his first novel. The poems were mostly bad; only a few years later he would follow Edward Garnett's tactful suggestion and abandon poetry for fiction. But the short stories were mostly bad, too, and the stack of rejection slips verged on the mountainous. As for the novel, even in the blind enthusiasm of youth Bates recognized its limitations, and it never left his own hands. In other words, Bates was "paying his dues" as a writer, learning by trial and error; and if the failures far outweighed the successes, he never let the disappointments slow down his pen. Indeed, he spent so much of his time at the warehouse in writing that in 1923 his employers saw fit to dismiss him for neglecting his duties.

Thus, in 1923, with few prospects before him and little desire to do "honest work," Bates did what seemed to him the most natural thing: he wrote another novel. It was called *The Two Sisters*, and this one Bates thought good enough to test the unpromising waters of the publishing market. As he expected, it was rejected by publisher after publisher. As he did not expect, in December 1925, it was accepted for publication by Jonathan Cape of London. H. E. Bates was twenty years old, and his career as a writer had officially begun.

Chapter Two
First Fruits (1926—31)

The year *The Two Sisters* was published, 1926, was a year of deepening economic crisis for England but great artistic promise for the world. In England, Conrad had died two years before, but Ford Madox Ford, E. M. Forster, and D. H. Lawrence were at the height of their powers and influence. With their experimental works, James Joyce and T. S. Eliot were expanding the potentials of fiction and poetry; and in America Sherwood Anderson and the young Ernest Hemingway were helping to transform the short story into a legitimate genre of its own.

Despite the spirit of experimentation that was shaping anew the literary world, *The Two Sisters* seems largely the product of an earlier time. Perhaps it is not surprising that the avant-garde did not find their way into Bates's conservative Methodist father's library. Bates recalls that at seventeen—in 1922, the year of publication of *Ulysses* and *The Waste Land*—he was reading Bennett, Wells, Galsworthy, Hardy, Conrad, and Maugham: a reading list we would expect to be compiled in the mid-1920s by an intelligent young Englishman with little access to the most recent names in fiction. Three years later, at age twenty when he was writing *The Two Sisters*, Bates was reading Chekhov, Turgenev, Tolstoy, Ibsen, Maupassant, Crane, Conrad, Gorki, Bierce, and Flaubert. Obviously Bates's reading interests had expanded greatly in the three years; still, most of the names on both lists are more often associated with the nineteenth than the twentieth century.

The one writer repeated on both lists, Conrad, is also the one among those mentioned who had the greatest influence on the twentieth-century novel. It was Conrad's influence which Edward Garnett—Bates's reader at Jonathan Cape and later close friend—detected throughout *The Two Sisters*; and though Bates revised the novel to mute Conrad's influence, he still left "evidence enough to show even the blindest fool that I had drunk deeply at the well of the author of *Lord Jim*."[1] Citing the innovative Conrad as the major influence on *The Two Sisters* may appear to clash with our previous observation that the novel seemed the product of an earlier time; indeed, Bates does employ multiple points of view in the novel, though hardly to the radical extent found in *Lord Jim*. But Conrad's stylistic influence on Bates is minor, at least at this point in

Bates's career. Conrad's hand is felt more heavily in Bates's exploration of loneliness and the difficulty of true communion or even the simplest communication.

The Two Sisters (1926)

The germ for *The Two Sisters* came to Bates one night when he walked past a large stone house with a solitary light burning in a window. The emptiness and melancholy of the house gripped him, and from that single germ grew "a work solely of imagination: indeed, it would not be untrue to say of wild imagination, the rampaging, highly-coloured, not always quite coherent imagination of youth trying to say something but not knowing quite what it wanted to say."[2] Reviewers of the novel, as does the author himself, point to the author's errors of inexperience with varying degrees of censure, although the reviews as a whole are hardly as dismal as Bates recalls in *The Blossoming World*, the second volume of his autobiography. Indeed, most are favorable and a few hyperbolic. (The most loyal Bates follower would hesitate to conclude, along with one reviewer, that the novel is "beyond doubt a work of genius."[3]) What most reviewers quite correctly sensed was a writer impatient of superfluous elements in his story, a writer more interested in and adept at creating atmosphere than plot or characterization, a writer whose prose was occasionally clumsy but often poetic in its beauty.

The Two Sisters is the story of Jenny and Tessie Lee, who live with their two brothers on the desolate farm of their father, Jacob. Jacob is the first in a long line of loutish, tyrannical fathers who populate Bates's fiction: "One could have crushed him, it seemed, between thumb and finger, as one crushed a grub, a parasite, as unwanted, repulsive. . . ."[4] Jenny and Tessie react to their bleak domestic lives in contrasting ways: Tessie by escaping to the local dance halls and Jenny by longing for freedom but succumbing to inhibition and becoming "too perfect" (60) to indulge in life. Both sense a chance for romance and escape in the person of Michael Winter, who bestows his attentions on first one and then the other sister, unable to decide in his own mind where his true affections lay. Just when Jenny seems to have won out, Winter is lost in a flood. At the end, with Winter and their father dead and the two brothers gone, the two sisters are left only with each other and their memories.

Bates fleshes out this bare outline with a half-dozen scenes of tension and power. What we do not find, and rarely find in any of Bates's serious works, are subplots, digressions, superfluous characters, or unessential matter of any sort. Edward Garnett singles out Bates's "artistic economy" in his foreword to the novel, and many reviewers agree. Decades later in his autobiography, Bates observed of *The Two Sisters* that "what had been left out was more important than what had been left in" (*Vanished World*, 54). This statement provides the core of Bates's writing philosophy; at his best—in the novel, novella, or short story—Bates will pare his story down to the essentials of dialogue, action, and description, leaving the reader's imagination room to work and thereby engaging him in the creative process.

Not all readers appreciate this type of writing, of course. One reviewer of *The Two Sisters* complains that Bates's artistic economy comes "dangerously near to the point of niggardly evasion."[5] Readers who demand a strongly plotted work would probably agree. But plot was never Bates's great interest. In "Thomas Hardy and Joseph Conrad," an essay published a decade after *The Two Sisters*, Bates insists that plot rates no higher than third in the novelist's virtues. Characterization is most important, with atmosphere second, but at times atmosphere may be even more important than characterization.[6] Certainly the reader of *The Two Sisters* is more likely to remember its atmosphere—idyllic with Jenny and Winter lolling on the flowered meadow, charged with imminent violence when Jacob is present, filled with foreboding when the flood rages—far longer than any character or bit of action.

Although Bates's emphasis on atmosphere in *The Two Sisters* is typical of his work, especially his early work, in general, his method of achieving atmosphere is atypical. Perhaps the single most distinctive feature of Bates's fiction is his accurate and artistic description of the external world—particularly the flora and fauna of nature. "What he sees he describes with near perfection,"[7] as a later reviewer puts it. But in his first novel the external world is only a shadowy background rarely described in any specific detail. Atmosphere comes to the reader mainly through the moods of the characters and through emotionally charged scenes. This occasionally leads Bates to some false steps—as when Jenny's father lunges toward her and for *two pages* she fumbles behind her for an elusive doorknob. Similarly, Bates's description of Jacob losing his balance and teetering over a stair rail takes over two pages and is unintentionally comic. Occasionally, too, Bates's prose—much admired by later reviewers—is clumsy and lifeless. But after all, the author was only nineteen at the time of the novel's composition, and instead of highlighting his infrequent lapses, perhaps we should marvel at his many passages of power and beauty.

While Bates's style and method will change only slightly, almost inperceptibly, over the five decades of his writing career, the subjects which he chooses to explore will be richly varied. Still, certain themes will be favorites of his, and one of the recurrent themes underscores the painful lives of the novel's characters: the difficulty of true communion between persons who so desperately desire it. Not only is spiritual communion denied the characters, for most communicating even on the most basic oral level is difficult. Jenny's brother Luke lived "an abnormally silent existence broken now and then by a mad frenzy, powerless to stop, and which cast him weak, tearful, more silent than ever, back into his previous strangeness" (50). Tessie is a girl of "retreat and silence" (84). Jacob shuts himself away in his room for weeks at a time and refuses to speak. Jenny attributes his actions to a "mere whim for isolation and quiet" (235); but the same could be said for her frequent need for the isolation of the woods and streams. Indeed, at the climactic scene when Winter first bestows a kiss upon her, she is filled with ecstacy but leaves without even attempting to express the joy he has given her. And poor Winter—he is more baffled by his own emotions and silences than are the two sisters. When Jenny finally asks him why he keeps coming to their house, he shrugs, "I know no more than you do. You want to know why I never said a word? I can't tell you that either" (187).

The results of this failure to communicate are at the very least misplaced affections and confusion. The extreme is personified by the grotesque, unloved, and faithless father, Jacob. Only Jenny and Winter achieve any sort of true understanding—through their love and engagement—but even this is snuffed out in the end by the pitiless flood that takes Winter's life.

Still, Bates's vision in *The Two Sisters* is not totally bleak, for the difficulty of true communion is only one of the two major issues in the novel. The second theme—just as powerful and pervasive but frequently ignored by reviewers—is time itself. As the novel opens, Jenny, a young adolescent, struggles to cope with a painful incident from the past: the death of her mother. She is haunted by the memory of a tune her mother played on the violin; and she alternately longs to escape from it and, when she does, regain it. Obviously, she does not understand what her relationship to the past should be—a question which will remain unanswered until the very end of the novel. Yet she does gain some insight into the nature of time when she accidentally drops her mother's necklace into a stream. She expects some dread hand to rise up from the past, but the water smooths over and runs on as before. As she stares into the water, she realizes not only that things pass, never to return, but also that she herself has changed, irrevocably: "Her whole body had changed! She had changed! Oh! she felt it, things were dropping from her even as the necklace had dropped, into the irrevocable past. . . . She had never believed before that there were certain things which passed away, and whose passing it was no more possible to prevent than it was possible to wish back successfully that necklace from the river" (44).

Although Jenny does learn something about the past in that opening section, it has not taught her to live meaningfully in the present. As the second section of the novel opens, Jenny is a young woman with few prospects other than spinsterhood. Her younger sister Tessie, on the other hand, seeks out life in the dance halls of the local town. Jenny admonishes her with, "I never did" (74), and that is precisely her problem. She has refused to plunge into the river of life. Significantly, the stream from which she learned a lesson about the past in the first section is replaced in the second by a fetid river: "foul and heavy with the rottenness that arises as a matter of course from the sluggish streams" (75).

The image of the river, frequently a symbol for both time and timelessness in art, forms one of the two major motifs in the novel. The other is the treacherous path which Jenny encounters a number of times: her fear of falling from the path into the water in the first section; the fear of falling on the dark, winding streets when following Tessie to the dance hall; fear of falling on the steep paths at night in the woodland hills. In short, Jenny so fears the false step that she fears life itself and is tortured by the inevitable passage of time. It is on one of those walks at night through the hills that Jenny finds her father, fallen and apparently badly injured, and sits holding him for a seemingly interminable period. The scene is emblematic of Jenny's plight. With her mother dead and her father perhaps incapacitated, will she spend her days caring for an invalid, with no life of her own? "Is all time going to be like this?" (100), she moans.

That Winter represents Jenny's savior from the fruitless passage of time is evident in their first meeting. She is so overcome by his masculine presence that she murmurs, "Please tell me the time. . . . I expect it's awfully late . . . isn't it?" (144), and then faints. But it is not too late for Jenny to engage in life. She and Winter finally break through their inhibitions and express their mutual love; and the river, which previously had reflected Jenny's discontent, now mirrors her saving passion: in a canoe the two "drifted on and on, beneath a shady roof of branches and from thence into the openness of the river itself, always through water smooth and bright as a mirror, measuring time by the sun, by their hunger" (277).

The novel and its time motif climax in the final section where the placid river turns into a murderous flood. Tessie, returned from a self-imposed two-year exile, awaits with Jenny news of Winter. The two sisters are potential antagonists, but they suddenly realize in their shared love of Winter and fear for his safety that past differences matter little; only "the happenings of the slowly passing minutes" (303) matter. Even this is not the novel's final comment on the time motif, however. The final chapter concerns a time many years after Winter's death in the flood and reveals an older pair of sisters living happily in the past: "Why try to bury a past of which two wonderful summers, wonderful alike in sureness and ecstacy, had been the more vivid part, though not the whole?" (316).

The Two Sisters, therefore, achieves a thematic roundness by returning us to the same question that plagued young Jenny: how does one live while haunted by the past? Bates's answer—to cherish the good memories while living for the present moment—may seem less than profound. Still, the time motif adds a richness to the novel which, added to his feel for atmosphere and often lyrical writing, overshadows the weaknesses of an inexperienced writer. More important, even though stung by several harsh reviews, Bates resolved from this first major publishing success[8] that he would never be anything other than a writer; and thus he turned to his true literary love: the short story.

Day's End and Other Stories (1928)

In general, British short-story writers of the nineteenth century failed to follow the lead of their innovative contemporaries in America and on the Continent—Gogol, Maupassant, Chekhov, Hawthorne, Poe, and so forth—in transforming the short story into a distinctive art form. Too often the nineteenth-century British short story was a ponderous, flaccid, verbose, all-knowing, all-telling foster child of the novel. But by the year of Bates's birth, 1905, British writers began to be stirred by the new, invigorated short story, especially in Ireland. George Moore had published his influential *The Untilled Field* in 1903, and by 1905 James Joyce had written most of the stories that would later make up *Dubliners*.

When Bates began to publish stories two decades later in newspapers and magazines, the British short story—with D. H. Lawrence, Katherine Mansfield, and A. E. Coppard leading the way—was in full flower. Theirs was a new type of short fiction, not merely the novel-in-miniature of Hardy and Dickens, but a form unto itself. Clearly, Bates's artistic

sentiments were with the new school. Again and again in his criticism
we find Bates bemoaning the sorry state of British short fiction in the
hands of such writers as Henry James—"that most elephantine of bores"
(*Vanished World*, 146)—and Hardy, whom Bates imagines intoning to
himself, "I have profound works to write. The longer and more elaborate
words I use the more profound I shall seem to be" ("Hardy and Conrad,"
238).

In the hands of Bates and his contemporaries, the short story became a
much finer and more demanding form for writer and reader alike. As
Bates observes in *The Modern Short Story: A Critical Essay*, "The story
described less, but implied and suggested more; it stopped short, it
rendered life obliquely or it was merely episodic; so that the reader, if the
value of the story was to be fully realized at all, had to supply the
confirmation of his own experience, the fuller substance of the lightly
defined emotion, and even the action between and after the episodes.
The short story in fact, moved nearer the film, and the two arts,
rendering life largely by suggestion, brief episodes, picture-sequences,
indirect narration, and the use of symbolism, developed together."[9]

This brief quotation is dense with doctrine that would surely strike
most Victorian writers as revolutionary. Most obviously, Bates allows
for, even demands, a short fiction freed from the traditional conventions
of the novel. Indeed, Bates speaks in theory for a form far more malleable
and experimental than he himself ever puts into practice. Bates testifies,
for example, that in the hands of William Saroyan, the short story has
"shown that it can exist not only without plot, which we already know,
without characterization, and without carefully created atmosphere, but
without any of the other rules by which fictional life is projected through
imagination" (*Modern Short Story*, 191—92).

The most distinctive characteristics of Bates's short story method are
three. First, it is essential: essential in that Bates at his best pares his
characterization, plot, and prose to only the essential elements. Second,
it is pictorial; "the direct pictorial contact between eye and object,
between object and reader" (*Modern Short Story*, 169) which Bates so
praises in Hemingway is also a hallmark of his own writing. Third,
partly because of the first two characteristics, it is inferential: that is,
"the method by which the surface, however seemingly trivial and
unimportant, is recorded in such a way as to interpret the individual
emotional life below" (*Modern Short Story*, 70). Add to these three
characteristics Bates's use of nature in image making, characterization,
theme, and atmosphere and we have the four distinctive elements of Bates's
short fiction from the 1920s to the end of his career in the early 1970s.

In *Day's End and Other Stories*, his first collection of short fiction, Bates exhibits remarkable range and polish, especially when considering that he had written all the stories by his twenty-third year. Some of the stories are particularly memorable, comparing favorably with the best from the hundreds that Bates published over this career. When the collection appeared in 1928, however, it received a mixed reaction from reviewers. A *Times Literary Supplement* reviewer, for instance, finds Bates's themes "rather queer and unexpected."[10] Another finds Bates's characters "too simply conceived and too briefly rendered."[11] Yet another, perhaps enamored of *The Two Sisters*, suggests that the novel is better suited to Bates's talents than the short story.[12] Even the harshest reviewers, however, applaud Bates's clear prose, the beauty of his settings, the sensitivity and honesty with which he treats his characters and themes.

Some of the unfavorable criticism might be the reviewer's reaction to a short fiction which works by inference rather than exposition and thereby places unaccustomed demands on the reader. Some of the disapproval, undeniably, is justified. The title story, for example, is beautifully written but too long; its unrelieved melancholy cannot be interestingly maintained over its fifty-five pages. Bates is two-and-one-half decades from the time when he will become one of the most prolific and respected novella writers in the language. The second story, "The Baker's Wife," is a potentially interesting vignette of a young woman's escape from a depressing marriage through a brief sexual encounter; but whatever possibilities the story suggests are spoiled by the almost comic caricature of greed into which Bates transforms the husband, who "growls," "sneers," "harvests" his gold from the bakery sales, and "hisses" repeatedly, "Wish we'd baked more. . . . Wish we'd baked more."[13] In "The Shepherd," Bates's descriptions of a raging snow storm are uncharacteristically heavy-handed and overly adjectival.

Such lapses, however, pale in the light of the heights Bates achieves elsewhere in the same volume. Perhaps a more profitable place to begin is with a story so beautifully simple yet fundamentally profound that Bates many times equaled yet never surpassed it: "Harvest." Like most of Bates's short stories, particularly the earlier ones, "Harvest" offers a starkly simple plot which can be summarized in a few words. A mother leads her four children on an afternoon stroll to a meadow at the top of a country lane. She watches the children gather mushrooms and berries in the deepening dark and then carries the basket home for them. Nothing else occurs. But beyond the scant action, "Harvest" is the story of a woman struggling but failing to maintain a romantic world of illusion; a woman who would be a child but is stunned by the weight of responsibility; a woman who comes to know, but never fully accept, her place in the cycles of life and death.

As in *The Two Sisters*, a pervasive atmosphere is an essential element in "Harvest." "Dusk began to cover everything, like an oppressing, luxuriant bloom. The trees weighed down heavily beneath it, the grasses shown dimly with wetness. From a great distance comes the sound of wagons rambling uphill. The reaper had ceased. Clouds with a dim amber light behind them had risen from behind the hill, and in a little while the moon would be up" (209). Here, as everywhere throughout the story, the setting is not merely a stiff backdrop but is a living, dynamic presence—ready, imminent. The effect is created in part at least by the author's appeal to several of our senses at once: the visual, of course, but also the tactile ("wetness") and the auditory (the "wagons rambling uphill"). And too, we cannot ignore the most obvious reason for the effectiveness of the description: Bates's easy, unaffected, yet masterful prose style. As one reviewer observes, "Words, phrases, sentences slip into the whole without a ripple on the surface so completely and minutely does one fit into the next."[14]

Filled with the beauties of nature, Bates's settings are especially distinctive because they are not merely decorative but are keys to characterization and theme. The children in "Harvest," for example, are identified with nature: running through the grass, their steps are "heavy and swishing, like the sea" (205). And their mother identifies herself with the happy abandon of the children. "She remembered looking forward with a naive eagerness as if she had been a child herself, to this time, each day, of irresponsible joys, of absurd laughter" (206). But the mother, of course, is not a child and has not, "for a reason she dare not let intrude upon her too often" (206), played with her children for some time. This is the first overt suggestion of conflict in the story, although the atmosphere which is "oppressing" at the same time that it is "luxuriant" hints of trouble in Eden.

Many short-story writers in the 1920s (and even more today) were fond of starting their stories *in medias res*: that is, by plunging their readers headlong into the action and conflict. Bates will occasionally use this technique; but the pattern of "Harvest" is much more typical, with the major characters, the action, the conflict introduced casually, with perhaps a mood suggested by that skillful delineation of atmosphere, then a gradual complication of image and incident until the reader is caught almost unawares in the heart of the conflict. Often the direction of the thematic journey is not evident until the very end, when the reader will look back and see that the pattern, all along, was just beneath the surface.

If we do not, therefore, know the mother's problem at the beginning of the story, by reading carefully we can see some of its manifestations. Evidently she is desperate to hold that image of her children in their pristine state. Romping in the field, the children form a tableau, with the tall trees at the edges of the field becoming the sides of "a golden frame, enclosing it securely there as a painting worth much to her" (207). Regardless of her desires to fix that scene forever, life surges on around her. Filled with grain, wagons rumble up and down the hill, and in an image which subtlely foreshadows her own problem, they seem to her to be laboring "under a great burden, too heavy for them, which made them groan" (207).

The mother, too, is carrying a burden, her fifth child. By force of will she can create a "fleeting illusion" (207) that the child does not exist, but the illusion is always dispelled by the certainty that "in a week or two . . . the other children would be saying to themselves, with simple, incredulous delight: 'We have a little baby!' " (208). The children's simple joy is contrasted to the sounds, smells, and agony of actual delivery, which are almost palpable in the mother's imagination. But her more fundamental fear is harder to articulate: "Sometimes the thing more awful than all of these, the inevitability of it all, made her cold with fear. It would be as if the night dew had fallen with unnatural heaviness on her alone, so that she felt cold in a world of sultry airs, of luxurious scents, of warm fruits and leaves. It became so that she was never deceived—that there was no illusion of miraculous escape from this new presence" (209).

We soon encounter the source of the mother's need to create illusions, plus the inevitable pain caused by the destruction of these illusions. "My little one, I promise you—no burdens, no troubles—only happiness" (209), coos a voice from the past, and then she sees the face of her husband. He had seduced her not only into the fearful burden of child-bearing but also into the illusion of his utter "kindness, his trust, his magnanimity" (209–10). At the hands of a realist and iconoclast such as Bates, such naiveté not only invites but demands deflating. Thus, by the time of her fifth pregnancy she has come to view this god-on-earth as merely "her husband, a being from whom she no longer expected promises and assurances" (210).

As evening gathers, nature assails the mother with conflicting images. One moment the trees heavy with fruit seem to be "uncomplaining," but the next moment the world is "overburdened with its own luxuriousness and fruitfulness" (211). She calls to her children, but they dawdle around a basket too heavy for them to lift. At their cry for help, "she hurried to them and lifted the basket with its burden of wild apples, blackberries and mushrooms. The children seized her skirts, her free hand and the handle of the basket" (212). This is the last view that we have of the mother: a woman literally hanging with children and the fruits of nature, not to mention carrying the unborn child. We might conclude that her rushing to take up the burden of fruit implies that she has done with the world of illusions and is ready to take up her position in the adult world of responsibility, and to a great extent this is true. But Bates does not overlook the painful realities of even this mature vision. At the end, the children's "voices fell loudly into the world of autumnal softness and gloom, disturbing echoes that ran from the heavy trees to the cornfields afar off. 'You carry it, Mother, you carry it'" (212).

Thus ends "Harvest," with the "gloom" and "disturbing echoes" as prominent as the "softness" of fertile nature. It is easy to see why those readers who like neat and tidy endings with all morals and resolutions clearly drawn would be disturbed by this story. Similarly, those who prefer plots composed of a series of actions marching resolutely toward some easily discernible climax would doubtless find the story lacking. But for those readers who enjoy a fiction of subtlety, inference, and indirection, "Harvest" represents a highpoint of Bates's artistry.

Not all stories in the *Day's End* collection would profit from such a close reading as we have given "Harvest," although a surprising number might. To be sure, little action occurs in Bates's early stories, and Bates refuses to expound upon what action does occur; but beneath the surface simplicity, image, atmosphere, and implication combine in a degree of complexity beyond that generally recognized by reviewers. In addition, reviewers often fail to see that Bates's range in this first collection—although certainly more limited than it will become in subsequent decades—is surprisingly wide for a young writer. Admittedly, most of the stories, like "Harvest," are set in the small towns and countryside of Bates's Northamptonshire, and most concern the common folk of that area: farmers, laborers, craftsmen, and their families. But given those basic materials, the stories offer considerable variety in theme and characterization. Bates, for example, treats stories of the very young and very old with equal skill. And he is able to transcend his sex to reach a sympathetic awareness of women's conflicts (as witnessed in "Harvest"). In addition, although only occasionally does Bates venture outside of his comfortable country settings in *Day's End*, when he does so it is with success. Two of the stories, "The Easter Blessing" and "The Idiot," are especially interesting because they are early examples of the way Bates translates into fiction his abhorrence of that detestable restraint against man's free will and unbridled enjoyment of life—organized religion.

"The Easter Blessing" is the story of an impressionable young lady, Helena, who is accosted in church one Easter morning by a starving beggar woman. In the slanting light the beggar woman looks to Helena disturbingly like a picture of a saint—indeed, she may *be* a saint—and to her pleas for food Helena can only "babble after the manner of the priests" (109). That the author means for us to take prayers to be an inadequate substitute for food is evident when Helena stops in the middle of one "as if she had been caught in an immoral act" (109). Still, the aura of saintliness about the beggar woman so intimidates Helena that she flees the church. When she has a change of heart and returns later with the food, the woman is gone. It is only that night when her husband returns home with the news of the old woman's suicide that Helena "with a sudden flash of horror recollected that while looking like one of the saints she must have been hungry too" (114).

"The Easter Blessing" does not have to be read as a direct denial of religion in general or Christianity in particular, of course. We could just as easily conclude that the author is showing us the dangers of violating Christ's teachings in the parable of the hungry friend. Only when we place the story in the context of a career of deflating religious pomposity and humbug does the theme come clear: the dangers of allowing superstition to blind us to an intuitive, humane response to need.

Bates's distaste for the too-frequently base side of religion is seen even more clearly in "The Idiot," the story of a simple-minded youth for whom the church service is a time of humiliation and terror. When he "steals" a coin from the collection plate—it accidentally falls into his lap—he flees from the church and attempts to bury the coin in the wood; but a raging storm keeps washing it up. Only when he returns the coin to the minister does the rain stop. In the end Taddo, the idiot, sings in his joy at this sign of forgiveness.

Was the storm an instrument of the Lord? Taddo was, after all, an idiot who consistently miscalculated throughout the story. The storm was a natural phenomenon which began before his "crime," coincidentally reached a peak as he fled, and "it seemed to him" (278) to calm after he returned the coin. An idiot would accept a religious interpretation of the events; so would a minister or a Methodist. The comparison is clear. We could reject this rather cynical comparison, however, and still be faced with the fact that the boy is indisputably innocent of any intentional sin, that he suffers tremendous guilt and terror despite his innocence, and that his anguish is caused by a religious orientation. Only an imagination perverted by religious dogma could produce the monstrous image of the heavens conspiring to punish an idiot Christ-like in his innocence. If we need confirmation of this reading, Bates tells us in his autobiography that "The Idiot" was inspired by one of his last visits to church, when his disillusionment with religion was becoming irreversible: ". . . so far had my contempt for organized religion advanced by that time that I spent the whole duration of the sermon reading a volume of Tchechov's stories thinly disguised between the covers of the hymn-book. . . . The next morning I sat down and wrote a story called, not inappropriately, The Idiot" (Vanished World, 179).

The reference to Chekhov is important, for the influence of the Russian master is felt throughout Day's End: the scant use of plot, the often seemingly random selection of detail, the use of "simple" characters, the reliance on implication instead of exposition to carry meaning. Indeed, throughout his career Bates's short fiction will be compared to Chekhov's more often than to any other author's. Bates also admits to the influence of another nineteenth-century author, Guy de Maupassant[15]; and particularly in the antireligious stories we sense what Bates found in Maupassant: "Withering observation, cynicism, merciless exposure of character . . . a powerful gift of irony. . . ."[16]

Five of the stories in Day's End—"The Spring Song," "Fear," "The Dove," "Gone Away," and "The Barge"—in addition to "The Idiot" have young persons as protagonists. Although none, with the possible exception of "The Dove," is as interesting as the best of his poignant tales of youth in The Watercress Girl and Other Stories (1959), they all establish a pattern that Bates will employ throughout his career. A youth encounters a situation so common that it would be ignored by most adults; but because of his naive wonder, he invests it with symbolic implications. Just as important, the youth's fresh vision allows the reader to experience the old in a new way.

Even more interesting than his tales of youth in Day's End are Bates's stories of the old. The title story, which concerns an old man about to lose his farm, is uninspired; but its very length and its place as the "lead" story in the collection show Bates's fondness for it. Three other stories with aging protagonists—"The Fuel-Gatherers," "Fishing," and "The Schoolmistress"—are less ambitious but more fully realized. "The Fuel-Gatherers" is an exquisite, touching tone poem reminiscent in method of "Harvest," with a profound vein of pathos. "Fishing" involves two old men who vow to recapture youth by once more fishing for eels, but in the cold light of dawn, neither is to be seen. Here Bates abandons pathos for a wry humor uncharacteristic of the collection as a whole. But Bates assumes the more caustic manner of Maupassant in "The Schoolmistress"—the story of a woman who discovers too late that she has been blind to whatever saving passion her dull life has to offer. Several stories in the *Day's End* collection do not fit into any neat category—such as stories about youth or age, stories dealing with one's relationship to nature—but deserve mention because of their high quality or because they prefigure some of Bates's major interests in later years.

"The Flame," for example, is a particularly fine story—the only one in the *Day's End* collection that Bates selected for inclusion in *The Best of H. E. Bates* (1963). Here Bates abandons the bucolic setting for a more distinctly urban one—something he will do with increasing frequency over the years. As we have come to expect, the story contains only the barest of plots. A young girl working in a diner waits restlessly for her date to pick her up. When she finally despairs of his coming, she agrees to work that night for another waitress anxious to leave. At the end the waitress sees the girl she is working for walking off arm in arm with the man who was supposed to have been *her* date.

Here again is the caustic irony which Maupassant would have applauded. But more interesting than the irony is Bates's use of indigenous material. Even before the bitter ending the vapidness of the diner is sketched in quick Hogarthian strokes: "The man in the corner smacked his lips, drank with his mouth full and nearly choked. A girl in another corner laughed, not at the choking man but at her companion looking cross-eyed. The cash register 'tinkled' sharply. Someone went out: nothing but fog came in, making everyone shiver at once. The man in the corner whistled three or four notes to show his discomfort, remembered himself, and began to eat ham" (148). The harsh sentences skipping abruptly from one impression to another help connote the superficial atmosphere of the girl's environment and lay the foundation for the disillusionment at the end.

Like "The Flame," "The Holiday" is a story with an "industrial" setting as opposed to Bates's more customary bucolic settings, and it is another example of a story that is a "mood" piece rather than the traditional rising action—climax—resolution sequence of events. Bates's mood pieces recall the "tone poems" that Sherwood Anderson had been writing for a decade in America. Although he does concentrate more on sharp delineation of character and structured plots later in his career, the mood piece will attract Bates occasionally even into the 1970s. "The Holiday" concerns a young father who becomes separated from his wife and child while returning by train from a holiday at the seashore. But with only minor inconvenience all are reunited and arrive home safely. That night the husband lies awake and remembers the holiday with "dull longing" and wonders, "Will it ever come again?" (160). So the story ends.

No one incident is of special importance in the story, nor do we learn anything definite about the personalities of the characters. The unifying element of the story is the peculiar "let down" mood, akin to despair, that strikes us when we have been freed from the humdrum routine of our everyday lives for a few days of carefree joy, only to return to the inevitable drabness of the routine again. And if the mood is the unifying element, then the major "character" is really the setting itself: the dreary stations where "the train ran in, to be besieged like a corpse by vermin" (157), the crowded train, and even the landscape, normally so beautiful in Bates's stories, but here "rained upon ceaselessly until the colour of dull steel" (153).

The particularity of detail found in "The Flame," "The Holiday," and the better stories in *Day's End* shows that Bates's method of creating atmosphere changed somewhat between the writing of *The Two Sisters* and the publication of his first collection of short fiction. In both the novel and the short stories, the atmosphere is shaped by the characters' moods; but in the novel, the atmosphere is tenuous and shifting, depending less on concrete imagery ("besieged like a corpse by vermin") than on descriptions of the often nebulous mental states of the characters. For instance, Jenny was fond of "weaving about her a spell into which had come the voices of the wind, the river, and the birds above the river" (24).

More important than the subtle distinctions between his methods of creating atmosphere is the more obvious conclusion that in *The Two Sisters* and *Day's End* alike atmosphere is still the most memorable element. Indeed, a decade later Bates would look back at these early efforts and recognize that he had been held in thrall by the "dreamy world of the subjective."[17] He would not be able to break the spell until after its enchantment had reached its most enthralling, in his next volume of short fiction, *Seven Tales and Alexander*.

Seven Tales and Alexander (1929)

By 1929, although the full force of the Depression was still two years away, England was already experiencing ominous signs. Unemployment in particular was distressingly high; and although Bates had resolved with the publication of *The Two Sisters* to be thereafter only a writer, royalties were meager, and he experienced the humiliation of the dole lines. For writers in many parts of the world, the Depression underscored what many saw to be the failures and inherent evils of Western capitalism. In the United States, for instance, the "proletarian" writers of the 1930s were prolific in their denunciations of the American politicoeconomic structure.

Socialist movements had been felt in England from the days of the Fabian Society and before. Perhaps for that reason it is harder to detect a sudden and distinct "depression" literature in England than in America. With his stories set far from the labor unrest of the urban centers and his themes calling more for freedom from moral restraint than for freedom from economic and political restraint, it is easy to see why Bates's fiction in the late 1920s and early 1930s is almost untouched by "proletarian" concerns.

Certainly, the world of *Seven Tales and Alexander* is far removed from the harsh realities of life in the crisis years of the late 1920s in England. Indeed, Bates's weakness for the "dreamy world of the subjective" reaches its apogee in these stories. To support this tenuous, subjective, "atmospheric" ambience, Bates employs a prose often poetic in its simplicity and beauty; and it is the poetic quality of this collection that reviewers most often mention. Bates has "what is essentially the poet's sensuousness," observes a reviewer for *The New Statesman*, "the poet's reverence for emotion even in its slightest manifestations."[18] Delicate, wispy, unarticulated emotions so underscore this collection because all the stories deal with characters who can hardly reflect on, much less analyze, their conditions. Three stories deal with the very young, two with the unlettered almost to the point of simple-minded, two with fantasy worlds, and one with a man living in a pathetic world of illusion.

Most of these tales are further examples of the virtually plotless vignettes that Bates had already mastered in *Day's End*. "The Barber," "A Tinker's Donkey," and "Alexander" show that by this time Bates was developing a fine sense of humor: a quality little in evidence in earlier works. "A Comic Actor"—with its caustic realism and ruthless exposure of character—stands apart from the rest. The comic actor of the title is William Twelvetree, an aging farmer who summons up the courage to audition for a village play. He falls in love with his much-younger leading lady and makes a fool of himself during the performance. When he returns home, his wife and children ask how the evening went, and he finds it impossible not to lie. They applaud his success, and the story closes with one of Bates's typically fine and ironic endings: "Then suddenly, not knowing how else to cover his confusion, he began to bow, gravely and with a trace of weariness, as he had often done at Christmas-time, smiling in a strained way as if indeed he had been some real *juene premier*, very bored and successful, at the height of his triumph."[19]

A world apart from the painful ironies of "The Comic Actor" is the title story, "Alexander," which earned high praise from many reviewers. Edward Garnett went so far as to call it the "high-water mark" of Bates's short fiction: "It is an idyll seductive in its atmospheric beauty."[20] The dreamlike, "atmospheric" quality of the work is appropriate from two perspectives. First, Bates is obviously drawing upon cherished memories of fruit-picking expeditions with his grandfather, Uncle Bishop in the story: incidents that he will later fondly record in his autobiography. Second, the protagonist, Alexander, is in that chaotic interface between boyhood and manhood when all experience has a poignant yet ineffable quality. Alexander's naiveté is undercut by a growing awareness, so that even though he may not fully understand the implications of each experience, the symbolic importance of the experience is fully felt. Thus, even though his trancelike wonder throughout the story is evidence of his immaturity, his awareness at the end that his state has been dreamlike—if not totally illusory—is a step toward maturity.

A sophisticated structure lies beneath "Alexander's" surface simplicity. The long story—seventy-eight pages—is divided into four sections: (1) the journey toward a rich old lady's orchards to pick fruit; (2) the arrival and picking of the fruit; (3) the settling of accounts and the departure; and (4) the journey home. Within the pattern of the journey, we see light balanced against darkness, youth against age, naiveté against experience, image against image, symbol against symbol. To add to the complexity, our original perception of certain characters and symbols will prove as illusory as Alexander's dream-trances. Characters whom we tend to see as polar opposites based on some rather naive scheme of good versus evil will upon closer examination prove to be "brothers under the skin"; and affixing traditional interpretations to traditional symbols—particularly those that are biblical in nature—will prove treacherous.

The story begins on an idyllic August morning with Alexander dozing beside his Uncle Bishop on a cart, the "overbearing loveliness of the ripening year" (15) all about them. The opening conversation between Alexander and his uncle provides us with our first balanced pair: Alexander's youth and innocence against Uncle Bishop's age and experience. To Alexander's warning that Ursula said that God might strike one dead for harming a sparrow, his uncle snorts, "Never mind what Ursula says! The woman's all nonsense and popery. Never mind what she says, the old fool. There's no truth in it" (18). But the polarizing effect is almost immediately dissolved: "Often something serious and mature lurked in Alexander's eyes; and frequently from the other's some childlike and naive light shone down upon him" (18). The two are delayed from their fruit-picking errand when Uncle Bishop gives a ride to an old crone, Annie Fell. Uncle Bishop decides to stop off and see Annie's father, and the decision is momentous for Alexander. He meets Annie's daughter (never learning her name) and is infatuated. He "became entranced" and walked behind her as if dreaming and "felt an odd desire to jump across the pond in a very romantic fashion and land at her feet" (31). They stroll through the garden, and she climbs into a sloe-plum tree (he is afraid to) and tosses plums down at him. Although he hesitates to eat them, the two loll in the grass and Alexander is in ecstasy.

This dreamy mood will dominate Alexander the remainder of the day, even when the girl "vanishes" (35) and he experiences an aching emptiness. Curiously, just prior to and immediately after his scene with the girl, Alexander encounters ancient, crippled Pollyanna, who stares at him "horribly and all her little black figure huddled soundlessly in the corner seemed to him sinister in its watchfulness and lack of life" (36). She appears as a cloud across the sun, an intimation of mortality, the weight of reality balancing ecstasy.

Alexander gets one more fleeting but inspiring glimpse of the girl as he and his uncle ride away from Annie's house, and he carries the vision to the old lady's orchard-surrounded mansion in the second section of the story. The Dickensian old lady with her packs of yapping dogs and paranoid fears of fire gutting her mansion and boys stealing her precious pears and apricots is a more comic version of the frightening Pollyanna from the first section; and she is a polar balance to the lively and youthful girl. Ironically, the old lady and the girl are the only unnamed characters in the story, heightening their "other-worldly" qualities.

Annie Fell's garden in the first section is also mirrored by the gardens surrounding the mansion in the second. More important, the sloe-plum tree (the Tree of Life?) from which the girl so innocently, generously, and lovingly offers fruit to Alexander is balanced by the "forbidden fruits" of the apricot and peach trees (Trees of Knowledge?). Uncle Bishop warns, "There's a peach on the wall, and next to it's an apricot, but there's never a finger allowed on them, the old tit, not a finger. Don't touch them, do you hear that?" (46).

If his uncle (a "Bishop") is the holy voice of warning in the garden, Alexander soon meets his counterpart in the person of Smack, the poacher. When he first sees Smack's black, beady eyes staring out from under an apple tree (of course), Alexander feels "an intense sensation of guilt" (53). At this point, he has done nothing to feel guilty about, but the guilt foreshadows his planned "transgression" at the end of section two and the sin itself in section three.

Smack's serpentine quality is underscored by the dragon tattooed on his arm, and he has an ageless quality: "Alexander could not surmise if this man were old or young" (54). Too, Smack's "sharp nose, black little eyes, and bony forehead" add to Alexander's feeling that Smack is "very, very cunning" (54).

But our tidy little scheme of placing Uncle Bishop and Smack at opposite ends of the pole on a holy/unholy, good/evil basis crumbles upon closer examination. Indeed, the two are far more similar than otherwise. Uncle Bishop, we saw, viewed the idea of a protective God as "all nonsense and popery" (188). And when Alexander asks Smack if he attends church, Smack's "face screwed itself up in contempt" (60). Lest we miss the point, Alexander reflects upon "how he agreed with his Uncle Bishop that it [the church] was all popery and humbug" (60). The similarities between the two extend further than their views on the church. Smack's crime in the story is hardly a demonic one: he poaches a rabbit and steals some fruit from the old lady's orchard. Uncle Bishop also urges Alexander to take a bagful of fruit for himself—"And don't let the old tit see you do it" (64). Similarly, Smack's cunning manifests itself largely in exaggerating the exploits of his children: hardly more sinister than Uncle Bishop's exaggerations about Alexander's prowess as a Latin scholar (68).

If Bates seems to be setting up a false pattern of religious symbolism, only to mock it almost in the act of creating it, this fits the thematic thrust of the story. The reader is drawn in to an illusory world, as is Alexander, and for both the illusions are destroyed.

After the meeting with Smack (the serpent) in section two, Alexander conceives the notion of taking a piece of fruit to the young girl on the way back. In section three, Smack appears once more—this time with a sack "of either apples or potatoes" (70)—and he sees Alexander as one of his own children: "You're like my son Squint, you are" (70). Immediately after this confrontation, Alexander refines his general idea of taking a piece of fruit to the girl to stealing one of the "forbidden fruits" of the apricot tree. But he is not struck by an angry God. Indeed, at the end of the third section the old lady's last words send him on the road with an ironic benediction: "God bless you" (81). Only through a willful reading can we see the old lady as wronged. Bates is careful to emphasize her pettiness; her act of "generosity" just before the benediction is to give Alexander a small apple "on which already the birds had been feeding" (81), a piece of inedible cake, and a penny. Again, we must contrast the old lady's niggardly apple to the shower of plums bestowed by the young girl in section one.

Alexander does, however, suffer punishment of sorts for his theft: the destruction of his illusion. As they return toward the woods where the young girl lives, his ecstasy reaches its peak, but Uncle Bishop shatters the dream with the cold practicality of the adult world. "Good Lord, what should we stop for? . . . It's a long way my lad, out of the wood and through the valley. A long way yet" (86).

The first three sections of the story, then, build a dreamlike ambience which the fourth shatters. Appropriately, the first section is in the pristine light of dawn, but darkness falls in the last: "Everything shaped itself by degrees of shadow and not light" (82). And the beautiful descriptions of nature are balanced by grotesque images after Uncle Bishop's refusal to stop: "A Great oak stumbled towards them like a malformed creature and lurched into the darkness" (87). More important, Alexander becomes aware that suffering and disappointment are distinct possibilities in life: "He felt that he would suffer deeply if he never saw her again, knowing at last, and for the first time in his life, the meaning of suffering as he already knew the meaning of joy" (85–86). Just before they reach home, Alexander realizes the immature nature of his ecstasy: "Then he would feel half-ashamed, half-foolish as he remembered all his secret thoughts, all his idealizing of the girl throughout the long day" (88).

At the end of the day, Alexander sits at home and recalls the day with mixed wonder and sadness. "The day had passed, the journey was at an end." He asks himself, "When would another begin?" (91). But we know that for Alexander from that point forward such a journey will be undertaken only in the memories of youth.

Catherine Foster (1929) and Charlotte's Row (1931)

Catherine Foster, published in 1929, marks Bates's public return to the novel: "public" because in fact he spent almost a year of exhausting creative effort on a long (150,000 words), ambitious novel (to be called The Voyagers) that was a total artistic disaster. His friend and reader at Jonathan Cape, Edward Garnett, called it "unpublishable"; and in a letter of rejection Garnett "put on a sort of Jack Dempsey literary punching act, using me as the punchbag" (*Blossoming World*, 57), Bates recalls. *The Voyagers* was intended to be a caustic comment on the falsity and decadence of society: a forerunner of *Ship of Fools*. That it turned out to be rather pretentious and juvenile is less important than its failure's effect on Bates's later work. It would be almost two decades before Bates would risk the time and energies required to write another novel on a subject far removed from his comfortable Midland settings, characters, and themes. When he did finally venture beyond the Midlands—with *Fair Stood the Wind for France* in 1944—the result was as spectacularly successful as *The Voyagers* had been unsuccessful.

During the period of the 1930s, then, at a time when he was continually broadening the reach of his short fiction, Bates was in one sense stagnating as a novelist. Perhaps *because* of the narrow limits to which Bates restricted himself, however, he managed to hone his talents to the point where he could dissect and lay open his subject matter with a surgeon's precision. *Catherine Foster* and *Charlotte's Row*—both set in small Midland cities much like Bates's own Rushden—are cases in point.

In many ways, *Catherine Foster* is a more sophisticated, more somber version of *The Two Sisters*. In both the protagonist is a woman who attempts to break out of her narrow, joyless world through a liberating surrender to passion. In both the heroine wins her love for a short, glorious time only to lose out in the end. In both atmosphere is the most distinctive element, although Bates manages a much sharper delineation of character in *Catherine Foster*. But perhaps the most distinctive difference between the novels is in the tone. The rather vague, mood-dominated atmosphere of *The Two Sisters* gives way to a harsher realism in the later novel. This harsher realism requires, and is achieved through, a far more specific, pictorial imagery than we see in Bates's first novel. Thus, we share Catherine's repugnance when she rubs her sick husband's feet: ". . . the chill, wrinkled flesh, like a toad's, the sharp grey nails and sour odor of sweat, pungent and lingering." [21]

Catherine Foster is divided into three parts. Part 1 charts Catherine's increasing unhappiness with her passionless marriage to the so proper, so practical, so dull Charles. Part 2 introduces Charles's wastrel brother, Andrew, and through an adulterous affair with him Catherine finally manages to experience the passion that had been so achingly lacking in her life. In part 3, Catherine discovers what the reader has been suspecting all along: that Andrew lacks the moral courage and basic human decency of even his stolid and stuffy brother.

The structure of the novel, thus, has all the simplicity and logic of a syllogism: (a) Catherine strays from a respectable marriage through infidelity; (b) infidelity is immoral; (c) Catherine ultimately suffers the unhappy fate of the immoral. The plot and moral are as mid-Victorian as the dreary house which imprisons Catherine. Clearly, however, Bates intends our sympathies and our moral sensibilities to lie with Catherine. The worst we can charge her with, from Bates's point of view, is being a poor judge of character. Like Jenny in *The Two Sisters*, she is merely unlucky in love. Our moral outrage is directed at the conventions of society that seem invented for the sole purpose of stifling the natural urges toward love and passion.

This reading is supported by the profuse nature imagery which suffuses the novel. We first see Catherine as she walks home from church; the gaudy beauty of nature is described in far more exact terms than we ever see in *The Two Sisters*: "A concourse of linnets, thrushes, sparrows, blackbirds filled the air with sweet pipings. It was intensely quiet except for their singing in the tall, green-fruited trees and the sycamores and almonds of the churchyard" (10). The beauty of the day causes Catherine to recall her happy childhood in the country, before Charles came and took her away to the city. Her reverie is blighted by encroaching Victorian houses—". . . the haughty windows, the sneering bright knockers on black doors and the circumspect red and white sunblinds" (11)—which lead up to her and Charles's house, more imposing still; and only by a force of will can she force herself to go "beyond those gloomy doors" (17).

Charles's respectable boorishness is captured in a scene shortly afterwards, when he orders Catherine's favorite pear tree cut down. If this were not enough to indicate that Charles is attempting to cut Catherine's spiritual ties with nature, Bates points out his "dislike of music, long walks and flowers" (22). Later, when his wife puts on a scent of verbena with the conscious aim of being close to nature, Charles recoils from her with a "How cheap!" (46), and she runs off in tears. She determines to dedicate herself to another, "who shared her love of sensuous things" (38). That person is apparently Charles's younger brother, Andrew, and Catherine sees their developing relationship in appropriately positive nature images: "Gradually, like the grass curling in a green spiral over his hands, the things he said, his quiet, earnest way of speaking, the pleasure in his voice, began to affect her, insinuating themselves into her experience like some fresh growth, a green shoot in some rank, neglected darkness" (100). When Andrew, lacking the courage to face an emotional or even economic commitment to her, abandons Catherine, her life becomes "a ruined garden without satisfaction or hope" (214).

Thus, Catherine is victim partly of her passion, partly of her bad judgment in bestowing that passion on two such ill-deserving recipients. A larger issue is involved, however. *Catherine Foster* predates our contemporary revival of the women's rights movement by some four decades, yet Catherine's inability to find happiness is caused in part by issues with which contemporary women's activists would be very much in sympathy.

Charles's dull complacency, for instance, is to a degree a personality trait; but at least in regard to his attitude toward Catherine, it is founded on the assumption that being his wife is her reason for existing. She hates many things about Charles, but "above all the slow, certain acceptance of herself, her love and happiness as unshakeable and unchanging things" (22). Later, when she dupes Charles again and again, her triumph is "feminine, composing and gratifying her" (216). Her attitude toward premarital sex is also markedly contemporary. After realizing her mistake with Charles, the premarital sex which she once viewed as "unthinkable and vulgar she now saw as necessary and spiritual" (23). Similarly, her fears of the stifling trap of domestic life have a contemporary ring: "Fears would assail her, again, fears that her life, soon, would become also one long conversation on baby-linen, illness, medicine, and the cost of food; that she might one day lose all her sense for light and freedom . . ." (30).

With its tighter structure, more exact imagery, more distinctive characterization, and carefully focused theme, *Catherine Foster* marks an advance over *The Two Sisters* in Bates's skills as a novelist. His next novel, *Charlotte's Row*, is another question entirely.

There are good things in *Charlotte's Row*. Bates's style is becoming increasingly pictorial, his imagery sharper and more precise. The novel is alive with a rich variety of characters, from the young to the old, the lovely to the ugly, the meek to the brutish. Bates's eye for the absurdities of religion is sharp as ever. Zachariah Corday, the Baptist baker, sadistically beats young Adam Vance for stealing a loaf of bread, then refuses to commit the "sacrilege" of putting crosses on his hot-cross buns. Several scenes in the novel are particularly well done. In perhaps the most powerful and technically sophisticated scene in any of the first three novels, we open with a panorama of a street scene. The focus gradually narrows so that we distinguish the rich variety of women gossiping about husbands, children, chores. At the end, the perspective narrows until it focuses on a young mother, sitting amidst the descanting matriarchs of the domestic world, her features twisting in horror at the dawning realization that the baby at her breast is dead.

Somehow, despite its considerable virtues, *Charlotte's Row* does not work. The novel is a thematic and structural mishmash. It begins and ends with young Adam Vance, and Adam is "there" throughout many of the scenes; yet he never acts as more than a mute, largely uncomprehending observer. Quintus Harper takes center stage several times in the novel. The second chapter centers on a debate over socialism with Quintus as the loudest voice, offering promise that Bates is finally expanding his range to issues concerning not just the Midlands, but the world at large. But none of the participants in the debate show a subtle enough grasp of the issues to make the debate interesting; socialism proves to be inconsequential in the novel. And Quintus, interesting brute though he is, never becomes the thematic or dramatic heart of the novel. The most dramatic situation concerns Quintus's daughter Pauline and her adulterous affair with the good-hearted Masher. Yet the affair hardly gets underway until halfway through the novel; and their flight to London, hard times, and eventual separation all happen "off-stage."

The one unifying, ever-present factor, really the closest thing the novel has to a protagonist, is Charlotte's Row itself. Charlotte's Row is a street sloping toward a railway arch on one end and shut off on the other by a brick wall, "like the wall of a prison. . . . A close, pestilential stench hung over the row, a smell of humanity living in a congested space, a stale odor of cooking and rotting filth, a breath of leather from a boot factory, a musty, powerful smell of malt from a brewery standing on the bank of the canal beyond the railway-arch, a stench of smoke, poverty and sordid living."[22]

But Charlotte's Row is more than just a street. It is a way of life, or rather a way of existing with precious little life or dignity or hope of escape. The emblematic gesture of the novel is the very last: Pauline burying her face in her hands as Adam rushes out to do battle with a world that is bound to brutalize him. The novel, in fact, is an anachronism: a piece of nineteenth-century naturalism without the redeeming political vision—simplistic and puerile as it often was—of the proletarian novels that were appearing around the world.

Charlotte's Row was published when Bates was only twenty-six years old, young as a man and younger as an artist. Flawed as the novel may be, it marks the end of his apprenticeship and looks forward to his flowering as a writer.

Chapter Three

The Flowering (1932—38)

The years 1932—38 mark a dismal period for England and much of the world, a period of crippling depression alleviated only by economies gearing for what promised to be another world war. Mirroring on a lesser scale the general infirmity of the nations, the literary world found 1932—38 to be years of relative stagnation. Most of the monuments of literary modernism—Mann's *Death in Venice* (1913) and *The Magic Mountain* (1924), Proust's *The Remembrance of Things Past* (written by 1922), Joyce's *Ulysses* (1922), Eliot's *The Waste Land* (1922), Faulkner's *The Sound and the Fury* (1929), and so forth—belonged to the past; and writers of the 1930s, with certain exceptions, of course, were still rolling in their wakes.

Even more so in England, these were uncertain years in literature. Hardy was dead; Conrad was dead; Lawrence was dead; the best works of Woolf, Forster, Ford, Kipling, and Galsworthy were behind them. To be sure, major figures such as W. H. Auden and promising younger writers such as Graham Greene and V. S. Pritchett still flourished; yet clearly the English literary sun was setting.

At the same time, however, 1932—38 marks an upswing in the fortunes of H. E. Bates. By 1932 Bates and his bride Margaret (Madge) had moved into the converted granary in Kent where they would spend most of their remaining years. At the same time Bates began earning six guineas a week writing the "Country Life" column for the *Spectator*: his first regular income of consequence since he began his writing career. In those middle years of the 1930s *Spella Ho*, the novel Bates calls his first commercial success, was published.

More important, 1932—38 marks Bates's flowering as a short-story writer. Bates did not ignore the novel in this period, certainly; the four novels published equal the number of short-fiction collections. Yet, even if we conclude that the novels are no less skillfully done than his previous three, they are hardly *more* skillfully done. Whereas he broadened his techniques and concerns in the short story during the 1930s, Bates seems content to use and reuse familiar characters (love-starved women), familiar issues (passionless husbands, the pain of poverty), familiar settings (the English Midlands of the late nineteenth and early twentieth centuries) in his novels. For these reasons, it might prove profitable to examine the development of these two genres separately henceforward in this chapter.

The Short Fiction (1932—38)

The seminal works of the modern short story—Crane's short stories (all written by 1900), Moore's *The Untilled Field* (1903), Joyce's *Dubliners* (1914), Anderson's *Winesburg, Ohio* (1919), Hemingway's *In Our Time* (1925)—were all published years or even decades before the period with which we are concerned. By 1932, two of the three great figures in the British short story, Katharine Mansfield and D. H. Lawrence, were dead, and the third, Joyce, had long since abandoned the short story. What remained to dominate the 1930s in Britain was a group of talented writers—Elizabeth Bowen, V. S. Pritchett, W. S. Maugham, A. E. Coppard, and many others—who wrote stories of skill and polish, yet rarely challenged or extended the possibilities of the short story as a form.

Among this number must be included H. E. Bates. Although from a perspective of short fiction in general Bates broke no new ground, the years 1932—38 mark a period of continual honing and expanding his already impressive talents and concerns as a short-story writer.

The Black Boxer: Tales (1932). As we saw in the previous chapter, in his early years Bates was under the spell of what he called "the dreamy world of the subjective": an enchantment that climaxes with the tone poems of *Seven Tales and Alexander*. With *The Black Boxer*, however, Bates felt that his aesthetic interests were turning more toward characterization.[1] Bates does not abandon his mood pieces, however; he will return to them again and again throughout his career. "A Flower Piece" and "Sheep" from *The Black Boxer* would rest comfortably with the *Seven Tales and Alexander* stories. And in "On the Road," "A Love Story," and "Death in Spring" mood rivals characterization and plot in importance.

Perhaps the best manifestation of Bates's new interest is "Charlotte Esmond"—originally published in a separate edition as *Mrs. Esmond's Life* in 1931. Charlotte is a graying, melancholy widow—"she looked like a woman to whom suffering came readily, but always as something to be repressed and borne in silence"[2]—who operates a small meat shop next to a theater. She distrusts the conjurers who perform there because

they deal in "deception," and she scorns her fat, lazy daughter Effie—
"she resembled some big, fair-haired doll made of pink-and-white
china" (87)—because she reads Sir Walter Scott novels and lives in a
fantasy world. Effie's condition is symbolized by the frail rhododendron
which fails to bloom outside her room: a typical Bates nature image.
Yet Charlotte's smug superiority to the artificiality surrounding her is
belied by her own hypocrisy—the smiling face which she puts on for the
customers whom she despises—and her dream of a better world than her
drab shop. The drab atmosphere, however, comes not so much from the
shop as from our growing realization that Charlotte's dream is never
going to master her hopeless, melancholy passivity.

Years pass and many things happen to Charlotte throughout the
remainder of the story: she becomes "interested" in a jovial traveling
salesman who in turn becomes "interested" in Effie; the two marry
against Charlotte's will; Charlotte transfers her affections to their child;
the child dies in a horrible accident while being cared for by Charlotte.
At the end, Charlotte is all alone, but in truth she has lost very
little: only Effie, who was hardly more than a source of irritation, and
her dreams, which were pitifully small. Perhaps at the end she realizes
that the door to life is locked against her, but it was locked all along,
locked because her personality—passive, hypocritical, despairing—
would never allow it to open.

"Charlotte Esmond" is the purest example of a character-oriented
story in *The Black Boxer*, although several others also achieve their
appeal through interesting characterization. The title story revolves
around a climactic fight scene (uncomfortably similar to Hemingway's
"Fifty Grand," with the aging fighter battling the husky young chal-
lenger, and the action turning on a punch below the belt); yet our
interest in the beleaguered protagonist at least equals our interest in the
action. In the highly praised "The Hessian Prisoner," action, theme,
and atmosphere center on an aging couple's transformation from a
somber, isolated, mistrustful pair to the joyful and loving surrogate
parents of a German prisoner of war who helps them on their farm.

"Charlotte Esmond," "The Black Boxer," and "The Hessian Prisoner" are the three longest stories in the collection, but even in a plotless
vignette such as "The Russian Dancer" characterization assumes primary
importance. The little that takes place concerns a supercilious young
magician who, much to his chagrin, shares a table in a railway station
dining room with talkative old Olga Ivanova (née Lily Miller). At first
immensely bored by her chatter, he is genuinely moved when she shows
him a picture of her younger self. Near the end, she advises him to

change his name, for one cannot be himself in the entertainment business. When he leaves on the train and she waves in farewell, he cannot look at her. We infer that by seeing the waste of her life he has sensed the superficiality of his own. Thus, "The Russian Dancer" invites us to consider not simply a situation or a symbolic action or a theme, but two characters who come alive and in doing so *become* the situation and the theme.

These four stories demonstrate not only that Bates's interest has begun to turn toward characterization, but also that his range of subject matter is expanding. Zeke (the black boxer), Johan (the Hessian prisoner), and the entertainers in "The Russian Dancer" show that Bates is ranging beyond the simple Midland folk of *Day's End* for his subjects. Yet those Midlanders are here in abundance, too—in "On the Road," "A Love Story," "A Flower Piece," "Death in Spring," "The Mower," "Sheep," and "A Threshing Day." And the same techniques employed so skillfully in earlier collections are here also: the casual, mood-setting beginning; the spareness of action; the reverberating effect of implication and inference; the refusal to neatly tie up all loose ends; the use of nature in image, atmosphere and theme. Add to these Bates's newfound interest in characterization and we have a short-fiction aesthetic which will serve him well in the prolific years of the 1930s.

The Woman Who Had Imagination and Other Stories (1934). This is one of Bates's most consistently lauded collections. Although a few reviewers raise the familiar objections about plotlessness or inconclusive endings, most point to Bates's fine delineation of character and atmosphere in creating stories strongly reminiscent of Chekhov and Mansfield. Graham Greene—a personal friend of Bates and a longtime admirer of his work—calls the volume Bates's first mature collection.[3]

Greene's contention may lead us to look for a more radical change of quality, tone, or outlook in this collection than we are likely to find. Here once more are stories of the very young ("Innocence"), the very old ("The Gleaner," "Time," "For the Dead") and the bucolic tone poems which we are accustomed to from Bates. The title story—in which an adolescent becomes enraptured of a mysterious young lady at a country house only to find that she is the slightly unbalanced wife of a crippled, waspish old man—is a maturer version of "Alexander." So too "The Waterfall"—which concerns a sexually repressed young woman caught in an unsatisfying marriage and being offered release (or so she imagines) through a virile, *macho* young man—is a more profound and mature examination of passion and repression than we have seen thus far in Bates's short fiction.

For other selections in *The Woman Who Had Imagination*, the designations "more mature" or "less mature" do not apply, yet clearly they would lie uncomfortably with the stories from the early years. "Millennium Also Ran," "The Story Without an End," and "Sally Go Round the Moon," for instance, contain only the barest mention of nature; and in the latter two especially the urban setting is as palpable a force in atmosphere and theme as are the mushrooms and meadows in "Harvest." Moreover, although many of the early stories end unhappily for the protagonists, in them we are often left with a sense of elegiac beauty in the midst of tragedy. But in these three stories we have hardly a hint of beauty. Instead, the reader encounters only bitterness over the foibles of humanity—"Millennium Also Ran"—or despair over man's ability to rise above his circumstances—"The Story Without an End" and "Sally Go Round the Moon."

The most pessimistic of these three, "The Story Without an End," concerns a young Frenchman, Pierre, who, like a flower, has been plucked from his home soil and forced to try to take nourishment from the sooty steel and stone of London. Pierre has come to London to work in the restaurant of a distant relative: the bullying, sadistically tyrannical Rosset. Pierre's physical degeneration during his stay is captured in a nature image: "he now looked like a plant that had been tied up in darkness and blanched."[4] Indeed, nature is still an important concept in this story of urban London, but important because of its almost total absence.

Pierre's only friend in London is the lively Yvette. One Easter Sunday—"There was no sign of spring: not even a daffodil on the tables of the empty restaurant" (25)—Rosset takes a holiday away from the restaurant, and Pierre and Yvette decide to sneak away to a park— "simply to walk on the grass, to see the daffodils swaying and fluttering in the cold April wind" (40). A sudden storm spoils their plan, but that afternoon they effect a spiritual escape through the most natural of all Batesian means—sexual passion. Unfortunately, Rosset returns and surprises them in the act. He fires Yvette but sends Pierre back to his old job, and we realize at the end that Pierre's situation is hopeless: "In his [Pierre's] eyes lay an expression not only of fear and sickness. They had a queer furtive, sideways look, that half-desperate, half-hopeless look, almost criminal, that dwells in the eyes of the oppressed and persecuted, of those who cannot escape" (47).

"Sally Go Round the Moon" also finds the protagonist unable to escape a spiritually suffocating London. In "Millennium Also Ran," the physical squalor of a young reporter's environment is exceeded only by the moral and intellectual squalor of his job. "The Story Without an End," "Sally Go Round the Moon," and "Millennium Also Ran" represent a degree of pessimism only hinted at in earlier works, the nearest relative being Bates's third novel, *Charlotte's Row*. Perhaps this "urban" pessimism strikes some readers as a more mature, appropriate response to contemporary life than the bucolic tales that dominated previous collections (and thus Graham Greene's assertion that this is Bates's first "mature" collection). But rather than terming the stories more mature or more skillfully done, we might profitably view the collection as one stage in the general trend toward increased use of characterization and more complex plots, a broadening of subject matter and setting, a trend that finds Bates employing more of the tools at the storyteller's disposal.

Cut and Come Again: Fourteen Stories (1935). Interesting though they may be, the bulk of the *Cut and Come Again* stories—plotless mood pieces set for the most part in the English countryside—seem rooted in the techniques and subjects of the early period. Indeed, were it not for two stories, "The Station" and "The Mill," one could justifiably dispose of this collection with little discussion. These two are interesting and fine enough, however, that they elevate an otherwise indifferent collection to the status of one of Bates's four or five best. Each appeared in three of Bates's collections—including *The Best of H. E. Bates* (1963)—plus collections compiled by other editors. "The Station" is the story of two truckers' stopping at an all-night diner, where the younger of the two is tempted by Circe-like Mrs. Harvey. Their interlude, no more than commonly sordid, is made fascinating by Bates's deft use of ambiguity in atmosphere, image, and characterization. By all rights the truckers' stop should be a relaxing and uneventful respite, but a strange tension pervades the scene from the opening image: "The leaves and the grass stalks were held in motionless suspense in the sultry air."[5] The station is guarded by the gasoline pumps, which stand like "idols of porcelain" (115), and it is just midnight, the witching hour, when Spike and Albie descend from their truck. The diner is ominously dark, but as soon as their feet grind on the gravel a neon light pulses on and off—*The Station . . . The Station . . . The Station*—and continues to "wink" at the characters throughout the story. Inside, the diner is hellishly hot and steamy—"The room was like an oven" (116)—and as the characters enter or leave the room they are bathed in the scarlet light of the neon sign.

Mrs. Harvey's mysterious, almost mythic seductiveness is enhanced when we learn that she sits in the dark—almost like a beast of prey in its lair—and turns on the lights only when a customer—her victim?—approaches. Even to her the light is "a bit uncanny" (119). With young Albie we wonder, "What's her husband doing letting her run the place at night, and just sit there in the dark?" (127), but are no more satisfied in our curiosity than is Albie by her brief fondling in the dark garden. The last image in the story only intensifies the ambiguity: "And glancing back again he could see nothing of the station but the red sign flashing everlastingly out and on, scarlet to darkness, *The Station* to nothing at all" (127).

"The Mill" shares with "Alexander" the honor of being the most often praised of Bates's short stories. It concerns Alice Hartop, a young girl abused by a harsh male world beyond her comprehension. Like the beast of burden she truly is, Alice is "leased out" by her family to help an invalid woman, Mrs. Holland, whose husband owns a delapidated mill. She finds life there amiable enough at first, in her own passive, indifferent way; but the pattern of water imagery that began in the dreary storm of the first scene continues, and we realize that her life is no life at all. All about the mill, for instance, are chunks of iron—junk that Fred, Mr. Holland, trades and sells—which have fallen into the water: "Rusty, indefinable skeletons of it had washed up against the bankreeds. She saw rust and iron everywhere" (47). Her days seem to slip by as unobtrusively as the rusty water: "Time seemed to have flown by her faster than the water was flowing under the window" (54). And the mill wheel races in the water as inanely and unproductively as her life flows by, since the mill itself has stood idle for a decade. The most significant water image for Alice, however, is the dead fish which she sees caught in the rusty grating of the mill stream. We cannot miss the analogy between the fish's condition and her own: "It was cold, and very stiff, like a fish of celluloid, and its eyes were like her own, round and glassy" (48).

Then she becomes caught in a trap just as surely as the fish in the grating: Fred half-rapes, half-seduces her one night, and then she accepts his joyless gropings night after night out of some dumb, passionless sense of duty. Only once does she refuse him, during a bout of "morning sickness" early in her pregnancy, but Fred knocks her down and takes her anyway.

Life brightens momentarily for Alice when Fred's son Albert returns from the war and shows her some kindness and attention, but any possibility of a romance is cut short by Mrs. Holland's jealous whining and Albert's discovery of Alice's pregnancy. (Poor, simple Alice had thought that she had "caught" Mrs. Holland's dropsy.) Albert, still kind, advises her to return to her parents, which she does. But at the end, on her way across the fields toward her home, she thinks of Albert and is stunned by a wave of tenderness. It is the first emotion of any sort that she has exhibited, and it is followed by another—overwhelming pain. Finally, she realizes what she has suffered and what she has lost, and the physical, emotional, and spiritual pain is acute. At no point is her agony greater, yet oddly enough, this is the most optimistic part of the story. The aspect of the story which causes the reader to feel such despair is not the circumstances of Alice's life but rather her dumb, passionless, indiscriminating acceptance of good and bad. At the end when she feels first tenderness and then grief, we know that she is capable of some sort of emotional reaction to events. Thus at the very end when Alice's eyes fill with tears of pain, Bates's comment is not a pessimistic one: "It was as though they had come to life at last" (87).

In "The Mill," plot, theme, characterization, atmosphere, and image are all important, with no aspect overshadowing the others, as atmosphere so often does both early and later in Bates's fiction. Bates employs all the tools of his trade in a degree of complexity, not contrived, as it comes perilously close to being in another story in this collection, "The House with the Apricot," but befitting his subject. "The Mill," then, is representative of the level of artistry that Bates achieved in *The Woman Who Had Imagination* and *Cut and Come Again*, a level which he will maintain in his next collection, *Something Short and Sweet*.

Something Short and Sweet: Stories (1937). Each of the three collections discussed thus far in this chapter has stories which rank with the best of Bates's long career: "The Mower" and "The Hessian Prisoner" from *The Black Boxer*; "The Waterfall" and the title story from *The Woman Who Had Imagination*; "The Station" and "The Mill" from *Cut and Come Again*. *Something Short and Sweet: Stories*, the last of Bates's exemplary collections from the 1930s, contains no story the equal of "The Mill," perhaps, but the collection on the whole represents Bates's most consistent collection to date. Only the rather banal "No Country" and "Spring Snow" fall far short of the mark: even the flawed selections from among the rest hold our attention throughout. In many of the selections, plot takes on a greater importance than ever before. In addition, half of the stories take place in an urban ambience, so Bates seems gradually to be relying less and less on a bucolic setting. Given Bates's love for the natural world, we should not be surprised that this abandonment of the country marks an increasingly downward spiral in the tones of the stories. Thirteen of the sixteen end either badly or ambiguously and leaning toward the pessimistic.

"Something Short and Sweet," for example, is steeped in such cynicism and bitterness that we might judge it a bit harsh even for a disciple of Maupassant. It is the acerbic tale of Mr. Malfry, an evangelist and Bible salesman who travels about with a young woman assistant. They peddle Bibles door to door and chalk scriptural admonitions on gates and telephone poles—illegally, obviously, since they speed off at the sound of any approaching car.

The Bates enthusiast will need no more background than this to guess that Mr. Malfry will hardly be a sympathetic character and that the young lady, if she has one spark of life in her, will be doomed to misery as Mr. Malfry's companion. Such is most decidedly the case. Malfry's oft-repeated maxim succinctly states the worst possible philosophy to Bates: "The worship of self means the rejection of Our Lord. Vice Versa the acceptance of Our Lord means the burying of the graven image of self."[6] Such words are anathema to one (Bates) who believes that the fulfillment of the natural potential of self is the only logical goal in life.

The story itself—more of a situation than a well-developed plot—represents proof in practice against Malfry's theoretical maxim. The bleak winter landscape outside the car, for instance, parallels the cold sterility of the philosophy being expounded within. The girl marches up to a potential customer's house "in absolute misery, in slush up to her ankles. . . . She felt the snow go right through her heart" (55). Yet, miserable as the conditions are, she prefers the freedom of the weather to the suffocating, life-denying ambience of Malfry's car: "Merely to get out was a blessed, almost hysterical relief to her" (53).

Malfry's harsh Methodism obviously has not found a convert in the girl. His sermons and her own spiels to the customers are "for her, a meaningless rigmarole" (55); and some of her religious "pitches"—inspired by Malfry—are unintentionally humorous: "God is at hand. At any moment he may strike you down. Have no fear" (56). We do not know why the girl became Malfry's companion in the first place—perhaps a sudden girlish infatuation, perhaps an initial burst of religious fervor that has since waned—but what she feels now are natural desires for warmth, food, a little genuine affection, certainly no desire for another sermon. "As he was speaking she felt painfully hungry" (54). But Malfry not only cannot recognize and thus respond to her needs, his religious fanaticism blinds him to his own. While the girl eats "ravenously," for example, Malfry "ate without pleasure, ascetically" (56).

The critical moment comes when the girl starts to don an extra sweater against the cold, feels a sudden sexual urge, and pulls her old sweater off instead. But the gesture is a humiliating waste. In the midst of one of his religious tirades, Malfry totally ignores her. At the end, Malfry stops the car for the girl to write another religious message on a telephone pole. When he hears a cyclist coming, he tells her to hurry, to just put something short: "God is love. Something short and sweet" (59).

The irony of the religious reference hits us with the subtlety of a bridge collapsing. Rather than pity we feel the same type of horror and revulsion at "Something Short and Sweet" that we feel when viewing a picture of the mounds of Jewish corpses at Auschwitz. The story is in effect a rather perverse variation of the *senex amans*. Here, the young girl is made foolish by her love for an older man; but despair, not comedy, results. Religious fanaticism has made one a passionless grotesque and the other the personification of frustration.

Most of the best stories in *Something Short and Sweet* are variations on the same theme of nature fulfilled versus nature inhibited. "The Captain," for example, is an almost painful reading experience: the story of abusive power, hatred, torture, and innocence defiled, all set in the lush gardens of a country summer home. "The Palace"—surreally set high atop the London Palace during World War I—concerns a lonely, frustrated woman's attempt, and failure, to find some spark of passion amid the hollowness of her life. "Breeze Antsey" might be considered one of Bates's very best short stories except that it so obviously draws on Lawrence's *The Fox*—both stories of two young women working on a farm and a man who upsets their "relationship"—that it slips in our esteem. In one of the best stories in the collection, "The Case of Miss Lomas," recently widowed Mr. Sanderson vacillates in his affection between young, vibrant Freda and shy, inhibited Miss Lomas, who is much more like Mr. Sanderson in her fear of passion than he admits or even realizes. Finally frightened off by his own desires, Mr. Sanderson abandons them both; Miss Lomas commits suicide. Mr. Sanderson fails to understand it, just as he has failed to understand any human motivations in the story, least of all his own.

"The Kimono" is perhaps the most well known and most fully realized story in the collection. The natural desires versus inhibition issue is more complex, less clear-cut here than in many earlier stories, and this contributes greatly to its attraction. And to those reviewers who intimate that Bates's solution to all problems is to jump into bed and get on with it, "The Kimono" requires consideration.

The story concerns the narrator, Arthur Lawson, who has come to London in search of a job. He becomes lost when searching for the very proper lodgings suggested by the conservative and religious parents of his fiancée; instead, he takes a room with Blanche, a voluptuous woman who wears a flowery kimono with nothing on underneath. A brief sexual fling ensues, after which Arthur returns to Hilda, his fiancée, whom he marries. But the thought of Blanche haunts him, and he deserts Hilda and returns to London and Blanche.

Thus far the thematic opposites are all in their proper places: Hilda and her religious parents on the side of the Forces of Inhibition and Blanche and her flowered kimono on the side of Nature. But the story does not end there. Blanche and Arthur's idyl ends when World War I starts and Arthur leaves for the front. When he returns on leave, he finds that Blanche has been sleeping with a number of men. Over the years he learns to accept her promiscuity as inevitable, but the situation still degenerates into a series of fights and squabbles, particularly when Blanche's drunken father returns from prison and periodically steals from Arthur. At the end, Arthur, now fifty, learns that Hilda is dying and wants to see him; he is too humiliated to go. Our last vision of Arthur is that of a broken-hearted old man, weeping for Hilda, Blanche, himself—weeping for what his life has become.

Bates obviously does not consider sex the answer to all problems. Sex cannot save Arthur's relationship with Blanche. Indeed, we might profitably view "The Kimono" as the obverse of "The Case of Miss Lomas." In the latter, both Mr. Sanderson and Miss Lomas suffer through passionless lives. But "The Kimono" offers a thematic combination of *Othello* and *The Sun Also Rises*. To paraphrase Shakespeare, Arthur lusted not wisely but too well after a woman who, like Lady Brett Ashley, simply could not help her promiscuity. It's the way she's made.

The Novels (1932–38)

Were we to read any one of the four novels which Bates published from 1932 to 1938, we would surely conclude that the author was the possessor of an economic and at the same time poetic style, that he could dash off scenes of power and tension seemingly at will, that his ability to paint in words a landscape in summer or winter, dawn or dusk, storm or calm was unsurpassed and rarely equaled. Were we to read all four consecutively, our conclusion would be the same; yet our enthusiasm might be tempered by the growing realization that the author chooses to exercise his virtues on conflicts, characters, and themes that vary little in any essential way from novel to novel.

Each novel is set in the English Midlands and covers a time span from the late 1800s to just after World War I. In each the protagonist is caught between two contrary forces, the land and time. The land is the often beautiful but always cruel mistress, immutable, ceaseless in its demands for bone-breaking labor and niggardly in its rewards. Time is the force that changes everything but the land, the flux that mocks our efforts and makes each aging man an alien in a changing society. Between the rock and the river, Bates's protagonists, every one, are buffeted, beaten, broken. Power, passion, wealth, domestic life mean little beside the inevitability of the two forces. The theme is a powerful one, and Bates treats it powerfully; yet the theme is always the same, and the treatment is always the same.

The Fallow Land (1932). This is not the best of the four novels, but it exemplifies the strengths and weaknesses of the type of novel which Bates repeatedly chose to write. Bates's strengths as a novelist are the same that we have witnessed in abundance in his short stories in this period. Rarely in English fiction will we find a novelist who registers so accurately and engagingly the sights, sounds, and smells—the entire sensory context—of English country life, particularly that country society as found in the apparently trouble-free years before World War I. Jess Mortimer's stroll through a country fair, for instance, takes the reader on a vivid journey into social history: "The bright paraffin-lights of the stalls and roundabouts blazed full in his face and he took a strong breath of vinegar and winkles and paraffin-flames and warm dust and trampled grass. The round-abouts were playing gay melodies, there were rounds of rifle shots from the shooting ranges and everywhere the rising and falling murmur and laughter of the big crowd."[7]

Bates's ability to register the colorful minutiae of the fair is mirrored in his skill at creating a host of varied and distinctive characters. The very number of distinctive characters who populate *The Fallow Land* tends, however, to preclude a more subtle portrait of any one. Instead of well-rounded characters we have men and women whose every action and reaction is governed by a single trait. Each character's trait is signalled early in the novel, and we never have to worry about, nor have the pleasure of witnessing, growth, maturity, change. Old Abraham Mortimer, for example, "has the same air of patience and servitude as an old horse" (13), and throughout the novel he will have the same dull perseverance and plodding constancy of an uncomprehending beast of burden. His son, Jess, "had a surly kind of strength" (12), and we know from the carnival man's early warning—" . . . look after your temper afore it masters you" (26—27)—that Jess's temper will be the deciding factor in his own life and the lives of those he touches. The one-trait syndrome reaches such extremes in Jess's two sons—the one frail and sensitive, the other coarse, bullying, brutal—that Bates comes close to caricature.

This "flat" characterization in *The Fallow Land* results less from weak writing—we have seen too many rounded, full-bodied Bates creations to conclude that he *cannot* make his characters multifaceted—than from the vision of the novel. *The Fallow Land* is perhaps the most purely naturalistic of Bates's novels—although others come close. Throughout, the characters are victims of forces beyond their control: the weather, the war, the passage of time, a single damning personality trait. Jess's uncontrollable temper, for instance, punishes all those whom he touches, yet none suffers for it so much as he. At the end, he is a broken, palsied, lonely old man. We see clearly from the examples of Jess's two sons that personality is not learned or acquired over the course of time but is bestowed at birth: thus, inescapable and unalterable.

The one character who seems capable of rising above the force of circumstance is Jess's wife, Deborah, the protagonist. It is she who suffers most from Jess's temper, yet she defiantly endures. It is she, a city girl, who battles hardest and longest against the grudging fallow land. Deborah seems most capable of growth and change throughout the novel, yet even she changes in no essential way. If she carries on the battle against circumstance more successfully than the rest, it is only because she comes better equipped from the beginning. From the outset we see her as hard-working, resourceful, and ambitious, with the touch of mental toughness and skepticism required to endure.

In the end, however, even Deborah is broken between the two opposing forces of time and the land. A city girl who knows nothing about crops or cattle, Deborah gradually assumes responsibility for the Mortimer's farm, largely through default, since her husband is a drunken wastrel and her father-in-law a feeble dreamer. She soon learns, however, that on the farm, "her every action was part of a fight against time" (52), and "the land was an opponent, a master" (70–71).

Bates's depiction of Deborah's life, and death, on the farm is a classic example of a latter-day experimental novel, in Zola's terms. We have the "test case," Deborah, who is exposed to influencing factors: a variety of single-trait characters, unpredictable weather, the eternally obdurate land, the corrosive passage of time. The point of Bates's experiment is less to determine *if* she will break—we know that time and the land are unconquerable—than *when* she will break. And this creates a problem. Up to a point in the novel we share Deborah's disappointments and rejoice in her momentary successes; but Bates seems so intent in piling calamity after calamity and misery after misery on her head that after a time our feelings become deadened. By the end when Deborah, old and broken, lies on her deathbed and still can talk and think only about work and the land, our sympathy has turned to impatience. A "chronicle of despair" becomes tedious if it offers always and only despair. A coffin requires only so many nails.

The Poacher (1935). At one point in *The Fallow Land* Deborah concludes, "We can't help ourselves" (164), a statement which might serve as an epigraph not only for that novel but also for *The Poacher*, indeed for all four novels in this period. *The Poacher* works on the same naturalistic principles that governed *The Fallow Land*. Luke Bishop, the protagonist, is the son of a rapscallion poacher, Buck; and he has inherited his father's skill and delight in poaching. It is obvious from the beginning that his father's "trade" has made the entire family social and economic outcasts. Our first view of Luke shows him wandering through the woods, being suspiciously watched by a river keeper. When he returns home, he finds the bailiff's men evicting his family from their house, obviously not for the first time.

If years later Luke marries and settles down on a farm," . . . beginning to see for the first time in his life that there was another way of living than the way he had always done,"[8] he can never entirely put his past behind him. His wife, driven by a mania for respectability, becomes paranoid about his possible return to poaching. Eventually, with a wedge driven between him and his family by his wife's suspicions, he does just that. An old man, he is caught and jailed for poaching. When he returns home, his family has moved, his farm-lease has elapsed, and he is once again an outcast in society.

When Luke forlornly concludes at the end that "he had nowhere to go" (303), he is realizing not only that he is outcast from society by his heritage as a poacher, but that he is even more irrevocably outcast by the passage of time. It is this theme which broadens the implications of the novel to include not just a disreputable subclass, poachers, but humanity in general. Bates, the omniscient narrator, first describes the changing face of country society soon after Luke begins to farm a small piece of land with his bride. Absorbed by his sudden interest in farming, Luke scarcely notices the machines that are replacing human and animal labor on the farms, the factories that are scarring the countryside with blackened brick, the "little chapels of corrugated iron and raw brick [which] were springing up, indistinguishable at a distance from the factories and tanning sheds" (202). Later, at the beginning of the new century, time still "travelled past him like a wind" (242), continuously altering the mode of life around him, while he slaves on obliviously.

It is Luke's leaden obtuseness to the changes which he should have been adjusting to all along that makes his return from prison such a devastating shock. Only when he returns to the farm and finds all the buildings which he had put up with his own hands leveled and two young men surveying the land—doubtless for a new factory or another row of graceless brick houses—does the full force of time's havoc strike him. The young surveyors signal "to each other as though in some strange language in another world" (303). When they invite him to look through their surveying instrument, all he can see is a blur. Obviously, Luke is deaf to the language of the evolving world, blind to its vision.

The Poacher is a more interesting novel than *The Fallow Land* in almost every way. Its primary appeal is in the freshness of the narrative itself. The life of a poacher is assuredly unfamiliar to most readers, and Bates's acknowledged skill in creating atmosphere serves him, and the reader, well in a succession of suspenseful scenes of midnight hunts, wild flights from keepers, sudden violence. But not only the general plot is more interesting than *The Fallow Land's* too-familiar picture of arduous life on the starveacre farm. The incidental details, brief vignettes, and occasional humor also elevate *The Poacher* above its predecessor. The language, for example, is more vivid, as when Aunt Hannah answers Luke's knock with a "Come in. I thought it was your great slommacking feet" (28), or when Buck Bishop, obsessed with athletics, appraises a prospective runner with unintentional humor: "And if ever a chap could run you can. Be God, I can see it by the way you stan' still" (58). We can sympathize with the abject misery of Buck's lodger-athletes when he rousts them out of bed before dawn, makes them stand groggy and naked in a wash basin, and pours bucket after bucket of cold water over them. And we can attribute only to sheer fictive genius the brilliant vignette of Luke, starving and exhausted after a run from the law, devouring a bowl of stolen hen-mush, his eyes constantly on the hens eating out of another bowl, Luke racing to finish the first so that he can steal the second.

A House of Women (1936).   In many ways *A House of Women* is simply a more violent, more sordid version of *The Fallow Land*. In both, the protagonist is a young woman who comes from a town environment to live on a farm with her new husband. If Rosie's husband in *A House of Women* is initially more dependable and admirable than Jess in *The Fallow Land*, still both women find their husbands unable to supply the love and passion for which they yearn. Quite early in *The Fallow Land* Deborah resigns herself to a life without romance; it takes Rosie some time longer—spanning a tragic, adulterous affair—but eventually she, like her counterpart, substitutes work on the farm for whatever life might otherwise have offered.

Once trapped into the day-to-day struggle with the sometimes reward-ing, often unyielding farm, Rosie's life is alike in every essential way to Deborah's, perhaps only a shade more brutal because of forced association with a maniacally jealous, invalid husband and vengeful sister-in-law. When husband and sister-in-law die, Rosie accepts an old beau's offer to join him in setting up a bar. Perhaps we might view this as a slight upswing in Rosie's fortunes, a chance for a brighter future, yet the novel has merely come full circle. Rosie was a barmaid before she left for marriage and the farm, and her life at the inn was not demonstrably less boring, arduous, and unfulfilling than life on the farm.

A House of Women is so similar to *The Fallow Land* in theme, characteri-zation, and technique that we can hardly conclude that it marks an advance in Bates's skills or interests as a novelist. Still, that does not mean that the novel is not worth our time. By this time Bates had become such a skilled, polished prose stylist that he could take subjects which were, considering his previous efforts, coming perilously close to the hackneyed and engage us simply by the power and beauty of his prose. The opening paragraph of *A House of Women* is a good example:

> The Alf Jefferys were turning their hay in the sunless heat of a June afternoon, the first rows of the first crop, the whole family stretched out like a line of dark and white washing across the river meadow. The five rakes skimmed the sun-whitened rows and fluffed them up and over, the undried hay a cloudy green and moistly fragrant. Once touched, the hay never moved, the wisps motionless where they fell, the heads of dog-daisy and buttercup and clover as still as though woven in a pattern of white and gold and pink among the pale green lace of the grass. There had been no sun or wind all day. The dark serge skirts of the three women never moved except under the motion of their thick legs. . . . The damp heat filtered down through a thickness of cloud that was never broken, and beyond the last hay-rows the river flowed slowly past like a stream of lead between stiff spears of summer reed that moved only with the little somnolent turns and eddies of water.[9]

The above indicates that, even while we wish that Bates would press on into new territories, once he does expand his novelistic interests, he will come fully equipped with the writer's *sine qua non*: the flair for language.

Spella Ho (1938).   Once again, in *Spella Ho* Bates explores the relationship between time and the land, in particular the effects of the Midlands' often painful transition from a rural and craft-oriented economy to a mechanized farm and industrial society: but this time with a difference. Here the protagonist, Bruno Shadbolt, rather than suffering helplessly through the changes while tied to a demanding but unrewarding farm, is himself an instigator and benefactor of the changes. That Bates's sentiments rested with the older, simpler, if often harsher life is clear from his discussion of the novel in his autobiography: "I saw in it not only a personal struggle but a piece of social history, a segment of the late Industrial Revolution that had marked my native landscape with so many soulless, hideous red-brick scars. In this landscape the remnants of the pastoral would serve to heighten the deadly nature of the new world of machine. . . . "[10]

Bates remembers *Spella Ho* as his first commercial success, and it is easy to see why the novel reached a broader audience than those previous. Dynamic, sprawling, crowded with colorful characters, enlivened by seductions and adulteries, brawls and riots, fortunes made and lost, theft, arson, and suicide, *Spella Ho* is easily the most sensational of Bates's novels published until the mid-1940s.

Spella Ho is actually four stories in one: Bruno Shadbolt's four successive (and sometimes concurrent) love affairs with women of various classes, temperaments, even nationalities. Three of the affairs end in death (sickness, accident, suicide); the fourth dies the most tragic death of any romance: mutual indifference. The one common denominator for all four affairs is the bifurcated quality of Bruno's love. Violent as his passions sometimes are, they are never as pure as they might be because, all along, Bruno has devoted his heart of hearts to a more enduring mistress: ambition. The dominant figure in the novel is not Bruno, certainly none of his paramours, but rather is Spella Ho, the gaudy, imposing, fifty-chimneyed mansion that rises from the hill above the indigent Shadbolt's shack.

From the first scene in the novel, when Bruno breaks in to the empty mansion to steal coal for his mother, who is literally freezing to death, to the last scene, when the aged Bruno is owner and sole inhabitant of the mansion, Spella Ho dominates the novel the way the squalid street dominates *Charlotte's Row* or the land does *The Fallow Land*. From first to last Bruno's every action results from or clashes with his desire—never consciously articulated—to be master of Spella Ho. This overriding desire prohibits him from devoting himself fully to any of the women who almost steal his heart, prohibits him from realizing that the means which he uses to achieve his goal, the stately old Victorian mansion, ironically produce the changes that spell the end for that nineteenth-century rural society: smoke-belching factories, blocks of dull red-brick row-houses, gasworks and railroad lines. Not surprisingly, Bruno's final success brings no happiness. Our first image of the mansion—"like a huge shell, empty and desolate"[11]—should forewarn Bruno and the reader. At the end, having sacrificed love, integrity, beauty—everything—for Spella Ho, Bruno stands a lonely old man before his mansion; we see him from a distance: "he had become one of the stones of the house" (414).

Spella Ho's theme of a poor man rising ruthlessly and singlemindedly to a position of power and material success while sacrificing happiness is not new, of course. In English literature it goes back at least as far as *Macbeth* and was especially popular in the American novel (*The Rise of Silas Lapham*, a number of novels by Theodore Dreiser and Sinclair Lewis) in the late nineteenth and early twentieth centuries. It has been revived in the 1970s in the mass-market novels often serialized for television. The theme represents less a new development for Bates than a fresh perspective on a well-cultivated subject: the fate of rural English society in the late Industrial Age.

In "Thomas Hardy and Joseph Conrad," an essay published in the middle of the period with which we are now concerned, Bates noted the irony of the English, a nation of seafarers and farmers, producing "only two writers of classic substance whose work has for its foundation the soil and the sea."[12] Whether Bates is a writer of "classic substance" is debatable; yet he is surely a novelist who, in the years 1932-38 at least, took for his inspiration the land. This, ironically, aligns him with Hardy, who suffers the brunt of Bates's aesthetic scorn in the previously mentioned essay. Not only are the two similar in their interest in the land and its people, but, even more ironic considering Bates's attack on Hardy, their techniques are strikingly similar. Bates is a more polished stylist than Hardy, of course. Yet both are fond of projecting their characters into a world of circumstance, a world of forces beyond the protagonist's control. Both broaden the narrative sweep to encompass whole decades, not necessarily to facilitate our understanding of character, but the better to analyze the forces at work on character.

In his autobiography, Bates terms *The Fallow Land*, *The Poacher*, and *A House of Women* (and he could have added *Spella Ho*) "historical novels" (*Blossoming World*, 91); and the label is accurate in two senses. Taken singly or together, the novels capture the flavor of the English countryside with the beauty of a Constable and the unflinching eye for detail of a Brueghel. In a more universal context, Bates shows us the effects of history, the passage of the years, on individuals caught inescapably in its undertow. Whether Bates would have written more novels on this theme is a moot point; history had other things in mind for Bates and the world: World War II.

Chapter Four
The War Years (1939—45)

The pleasant turn in Bates's fortunes which began with the success of *Spella Ho* in England in 1938 climaxed later that year when he traveled to the United States to oversee serialization of the novel for the *Atlantic Monthly*. But Bates's prospects contrasted sharply with England's and Western Europe's. The desperate years of world-wide depression were evolving into the even more disheartening specter of an inevitable world war. In 1939, the war between England and Germany was officially declared; and even though its first manifestations were sedentary, Bates did not have to be a prophet to foresee its imminent cataclysm.

Considering the looming war and the prolonged economic depression, it is not surprising that Bates's vision grows increasingly bleak throughout the 1930s. As we have seen, the landscape becomes more and more urban, the circumstances impinging upon the free and passionate life more and more inescapable, psychological inhibitions choking out natural impulses increasingly the rule. Yet at the same time that Bates's vision becomes despairing, his most joyous, life-affirming, recurrent character appears: Uncle Silas.

My Uncle Silas: Stories (1939)

In his preface to *My Uncle Silas: Stories*[1] Bates recalls that when he wrote the first of the stories, "The Lily," he had no thought of a series of stories about his protagonist. The public response was so great, however, and Silas was obviously so congenial a spokesman for Bates's own philosophy, that he resurrected the lusty old sinner again and again. Bates's comments on the dual nature of the English personality serve as a fitting introduction to Silas: "The English character still contains in it, generally, very strong elements of the Puritans. You see it at its fiercest, in conflict, in artists like D. H. Lawrence, at its pettiest in magistrates who remonstrate with young ladies who appear in court without stockings or reprove young men who appear in sports coats. But now and then the stream of the original Adam, rich and lusty and robust, comes straight through, undiluted and unpurified. This strong original devilishness sprouts up in characters like my Uncle Silas. . . ."[2]

With the Puritan on one side of the ideological fence and "rich and lusty and robust" Silas on the other, it is easy to see why Silas takes on an almost mythically heroic stature in Bates's stories. Bates hardly attempts to conceal his fondness for his creation: "Certainly there was no strain of the Puritan in my Uncle Silas, who got gloriously and regularly drunk, loved food and ladies and good company, was not afraid to wear a huge and flamboyant buttonhole, told lies, got the better of his fellow man whenever the chance offered itself, used a scythe like an angel, was a wonderful gardener, took the local lord's pheasants, and yet succeeded in remaining an honest, genuine and lovable character" (*Uncle Silas,* 11).

The prototype for Silas was a distant relative of Bates's, Joseph Betts. Many of the situations in the Silas tales are patterned, apparently, after incidents in Bett's life. Others "have been inspired by that sort of apocryphal legend which is the inheritance of every country child who keeps his ears cocked when men are talking" (*Uncle Silas*, 11). Thus, the dual sources account in part for the delightful mixture of comic realism and tall-tale myth.

"Squat, misshapen, wickedly ugly, he looked something like a gargoyle . . . ," Silas is Bates's great comic creation. The stories are so fresh and charming that one hesitates to analyze them. But in truth, no great amount of analysis of these simple tales is possible. All the tales are narrated by Silas's great-nephew, who recalls escapades that he witnessed when very young—"The Revelation," "The Wedding"—or reports incidents of Silas's younger days—"A Silas Idyll," "Silas and Goliath," and so forth. Most of the latter have been passed down to him by Silas himself, whose penchant for exaggeration is exceeded only by his great thirst and lust. Often the narrator is as skeptical of, and as entertained by, the wild tales as is the reader. Most of the tales fit loosely into one or a combination of three patterns: (1) Silas in a sexual encounter ("The Lily," "The Revelation," "Finger Wet, Finger Dry"); (2) Silas in a bragging, drinking, shooting, or athletic match with someone who is almost, but not quite, as great a blowhard as Silas himself ("A Funny Thing," "The Shooting Party," "Silas and Goliath," "The Race"); and (3) "rakish and wicked" (*Uncle Silas*, 23) Silas in some orgiastic situation carefully calculated to outrage his Puritanical antagonist ("The Revelation," "The Wedding," "The Sow and Silas," "Silas the Good," "A Silas Idyll").

Bates cited two sources for the Silas stories—Joseph Betts and local legend—but some literary influences are distinctly evident also. Bates obviously owes much, for instance, to the American local-color tradition of the nineteenth century. Like the local-color tales, the Silas stories

sparkle with indigenous characters often exaggerated to comic proportion, idiomatic dialogue, and situations which smack of the tall tale. In
"Finger Wet, Finger Dry," for example, Silas claims to have been
playing "find the duck eggs" with friend Sam's wife—she hid them "in
the oven. In the bed. Oh, she was a tartar. She was hot" (65)—when Sam
returned unexpectedly. Silas hid in the basement. He was forced to
remain there three weeks and became so ravenous that he resorted to
eating stewed nails. Offering proof to the young but skeptical narrator,
Silas shows him his yellow, broken teeth: "That's where women land
you" (68), he sighs.

The most obvious literary influence on the stories is Mark Twain,
whom Bates had read and appreciated. In "How to Tell a Story," Twain
divided stories into the "humorous" (the American), the "witty" (French),
and the "comic" (English): "The humorous story depends for its effect
upon the *manner* of the telling; the comic story and the witty story upon
the *matter*."[3] Although there is certainly a good deal of funny matter in
the Silas tales, the lion's share of the charm resides in the manner of
presentation. One cannot examine Bates's manner without being reminded of Twain.

For instance, all of the tales revolve around a central incident—often
indicated by the title—but, as in Twain, the reader arrives at that
incident only by a circuitous route. We must allow Silas time to argue
about an irrelevant detail with an eavesdropper, sip a few glasses of
cowslip wine, ramble through a few anecdotes, interpolate a tale or two.
The central incident in "Finger Wet, Finger Dry" is Silas's escapade
with Sam's wife, but the story is half over before the incident is even
introduced. One cannot help but be reminded of Twain's rambling and
illusive tale of Blaine's grandfather's old ram (found under various titles)
from *Roughing It*.

In addition, as does Twain, Bates employs exaggeration in character
and image to humorous effect. The "female" in "Silas the Good," for
example, is ugly to the point of caricature: "She was very pale, updrawn
and skinny, with a face, as Silas described it, like a turnip lantern with
the handle out. She seemed to have size nine boots on and from under her
thick black skirt Silas caught a glimpse of an amazing knickerbocker leg,
baggy, brown in colour, and about the size of an airship" (114).

Hand in hand with caricature is the exaggerated image, as in "The
Shooting Party," where a drunken Silas tries to fire at a turkey, "the gun
wavering about as though held by a man with St. Vitus's dance" (105).
And certain touches defy analysis but bear the mark of Twain's unmis-
takable wry irony; thus, the rifle in "The Shooting Party": "It was a good

gun, except for one thing. There were times when it would not go off. The trigger would jam and nothing on earth would move it. Finally, just as you had given it up as a bad job, it suddenly went off and blew the roof out or killed a cow or something. Otherwise a fine gun" (103).

Thematically, Twain's humorous pieces nearly always explode some romantic notion, and the iconoclast Silas in the same way runs rough-shod over the Puritanical, nay-saying world. Ironically, in battling the inhibiting myths of religion and false morality, Silas himself becomes the closest thing to a figure of mythic proportions in Bates's work. His heroic stature is necessary in a world where—as we see so often in Bates's fiction—circumstance so relentlessly impinges on nature. In future Bates collections circumstance will win out again and again; but in the bleakest times Silas will be resurrected—a gleam in his eye, lust in his heart, and a mug of beer in his hand—to do uproarious battle with life.

The Flying Goat (1939) and The Beauty of the Dead and Other Stories (1940)

Unquestionably, the Uncle Silas stories represent one of the memorable achievements in Bates's canon. Coming at the beginning of the war years, however, the collection should not mislead us into expecting this period to be a productive one for Bates. The Flying Goat is without a doubt Bates's most forgettable work. Following almost immediately, The Beauty of the Dead and Other Stories is more interesting but falls far short of the high quality achieved in the four collections published in the mid-1930s.

What is the reason for Bates's decline in effectiveness? Any answer would be largely conjecture, but several circumstances might be relevant. For one thing, by 1940 Bates had been producing volumes of fiction at the rate of better than one a year for fourteen years. Although he had reached the point where he could support himself through writing, financial security was still little more than a dream. Thus, fourteen years of continuous literary effort rewarded him with little money and little recognition beyond a small following.

That lack of money and recognition might have affected Bates is purely guesswork, but that by 1939 he was in a deep crisis of literary self-doubt is not. During 1938 and 1939, greatly influenced by Douglas Reed's prophetic *Insanity Fair*, Bates devoted considerable time and energies to an antiwar novel which he hoped and truly felt to be his best effort. But when Edward Garnett and Rupert Hart-Davis—two old friends whose judgment Bates valued highly—read the manuscript, their criticism was merciless. Bates recalls his depression: "In this new and embittering disappointment, entirely of my own making, I could only ask myself if I really knew, after all, what I was doing as a writer? Was there in me some leaden vein of obtuseness that would never be taught, would never learn? With utter melancholy I could only tell myself that there must be." [4] Bates's confidence was so shaken that for a time he considered abandoning the novel, and for years thereafter he "found it impossible to work creatively" (*Blossoming World*, 158).

Bates's despair over his stillborn novel was only deepened by his gloom over the approaching war. He sensed quite correctly that his life-style was about to be drastically altered: "I was at a football match when I heard its [war's] cruel, sanctimonious, funereal knell and I wasn't far away from the impulse to shoot, if not myself at least the guardians of 'peace in our time.' I thought greatly then of my children: my two beautiful daughters and my young son, impeccable as always in his cream shantung jacket. My world, which had at last seemed about to blossom to the full, was instead to be blighted, together with that of unlimited millions of others" (*Blossoming World*, 146).

Bates's bitterness over his about-to-be-blighted world is reflected in the large number of stories in *The Beauty of the Dead* which explore the cruel effects of time, the tragic distance between what was and what is, the changing conditions faced by the English on social, economic, and personal levels. In "The Bridge," for example, the conflict between two sisters is initiated by the construction of a new steel and concrete bridge, replacing the old "humpbacked" one, which causes the main road to bypass their home and jeopardizes plans for their rooming house. "Fuchsia"—a less ambitious but much finer story than "The Bridge"— concerns an unemployed and "henpecked" little man who wanders the streets of London stung by memories of a more respectable past: "Fragmentary memories of the past flashed across his mind exactly as the sparks flashed along the elevated tram-wires. He did not consciously think of things as they had been. It was not possible for him to grasp the pictures of himself, independent, in regular work, able to demand a thing and pay for it or ask a question and get an answer, before despondence absorbed and extinguished them again." [5] Time's alteration is a less obvious theme in "The Ferry," but it appears nevertheless. Richardson, the protagonist, has come to an inn to do some fishing but finds the fishing poorer than he had been led to believe. The innkeeper claims that the fishing was once excellent, but the river has been fished out over the years, and industry has polluted it. "Nothing left but water-rats and gudgeon" (64), she concludes.

The most interesting and unusual analysis of the changing economic and social face of rural England is found in "The Earth." "The Earth" is unusual because it concerns an idiot who is *not* pictured at all sympathetically. Indeed, the idiot in this case embodies the antagonistic side of the theme. Benjy is the idiot son of the Johnsons, a farming family, and like Faulkner's Benjy is in his early thirties. But there the resemblance ends. Benjy Johnson is an "idiot savant" of sorts at raising and selling chickens. He is so successful that he saves enough to buy the farm next to his parents', and then years later when the parents' farm is up for sale (and they cannot afford to buy it) he purchases it also. He moves in with his ugly little wife, Florence, takes over the master bedroom from his parents, and in the end forces them to move out entirely.

In "The Earth" we find Benjy and his parents on opposite sides of social and economic change. Instead of viewing Benjy as simpleminded, perhaps we should view him as rapaciously single-minded. His entire psyche devoted to the war between profit and loss, Benjy is modern, acquisitive, corporate man in his purest state, without emotion or sentiment. His take-over of his parents's home has all the ruthless logic of a bank foreclosure: "This is our house now. We want it. I bought the house and I want it now" (210).

But the Johnsons share in their own downfall. Lazy, short-sighted, impracticably religious, "they had put rather more value on faith than sweat." Mr. Johnson had been a minister, and he "talked so much that he must have had an idea that the earth, designed, created, and nourished by God, would take care of itself" (202). Once again we see the falsity and injuriousness of religion. Even the world of nature seems openly to attack Mr. Johnson's faith: "While he talked the thistles seeded and choked his wheat, rabbits broke in and gnawed his cabbages, storms smashed his standing corn" (202).

If the Johnsons represent a way of life and a way of thinking which have outlived their usefulness in a world where profit and loss are the sole determinants of viability, their end is truly symbolic. Benjy takes them to the city, where they live out their days in an apartment, having lost the earth forever.

Almost without exception, the stories in *The Beauty of the Dead* are more interesting than those in *The Flying Goat*, yet they fall far short of the better efforts in the earlier collections. Most, if not all, are flawed works. The title story, for example, explores one aspect of the same theme that we have seen so often in Bates's novels and stories—the tragedy of devoting oneself to things and not passion—yet it lacks the redeeming subtlety and complexity which we saw in "The Mill" or "The Kimono" or a dozen others. Worse, Bates lapses again and again into a regrettable discursiveness that is diametrically opposed to the artistic virtues that he defends in theory and previously executed so admirably in practice. Thus, the plot and imagery of "The Beauty of the Dead" provide abundant support for the theme; yet Bates appears desperate that we not miss the point: "They had lived alone together for a long time. The furniture and glass had taken the place, gradually, of people and fields, friends and outside things. No one could understand how they felt, how he himself felt, about the beauty of things for which they had starved and cheated themselves" (19).

At this point in Bates's career the freshness and vigor seem to be largely absent from his writing. One could hardly guess that in just a few years the measure of fame and financial security that he long had deserved would be his.

The Greatest People in the World and Other Stories (1942) and *How Sleep the Brave and Other Stories* (1943)

The cause of the radical turn in Bates's fortunes was—as he describes it in *The Blossoming World*—nothing less than the "hand of fate." In the summer of 1941, Bates's exemption from the armed forces was about to expire, and he petitioned his old friend David Garnett in the British Air Ministry for help in obtaining some special commission. Eventually, through the help of Garnett and others, Bates was commissioned into the Royal Air Force as strictly a short-story writer—the only man so appointed to such a unique position in the British armed forces.

Bates's specific task was to write short stories about R.A.F. bomber pilots, and his assignments took him to the Continent, India, and Burma. The eventual result was two slender volumes: *The Greatest People in the World and Other Stories* and *How Sleep the Brave and Other Stories*, published under the pseudonym Flying Officer 'X' and later collected as *The Stories of Flying Officer 'X'* (1952).

The reception of the Flying Officer 'X' stories far exceeded the Air Ministry's or Bates's wildest dreams. The identity of Flying Officer 'X' soon became common knowledge, and Bates's fame—in his own home-land at least—was assured. Rarely does a review of one of the volumes contain anything other than the most extravagant praise. Bates was justifiably proud of his contribution to the morale of the British people and fighting men during the war, and although the stories can hardly compare on purely aesthetic grounds to his earlier efforts, they are surprisingly good for commissioned propaganda pieces.

In each of the stories Bates sketches in a few deft strokes easily recognizable military types: the battle-loving Texan, the naive but brave youth from Kalgoolie, the slightly cynical French veteran. In each the protagonist—pilot, parent, or girl back home—faces some obstacle—cowardice, bad luck, grief, endless waiting—and overcomes it through strength of character. If the cynical post-Vietnam-era reader might find the consistently understated "good show" courage a bit cloying and a bit of a sentimental pose, surely it is preferable to the inflated bravado in which a lesser writer might have indulged.

For his efforts in creating the immensely popular Flying Officer 'X,' Bates received not a farthing above his wage as an R.A.F. officer, a circumstance that led him to break his long relationship with his publisher, Jonathan Cape, and establish a happier one with Michael Joseph. What the stories did do was make his name known to an expanded audience, which in turn made possible a series of popular novels over the next several years.

Fair Stood the Wind for France (1944)

Fair Stood the Wind for France was the first of a series of novels drawing upon Bates's experiences, observations, and "eavesdropping" (Bates's term) while working for the Air Ministry in World War II. The English edition still bore the pseudonym Flying Officer 'X'; but Bates had a new publisher, Michael Joseph, and a new agent, Laurence Pollinger, and from this volume Bates profited handsomely. With an advance on the novel, plus serialization rights in England and America, for the first time in his life Bates was free of financial anxiety.[6]

Fair Stood the Wind for France was not only financially successful but was well received by most reviewers. One comment, by Fowler Hill, a *New York Times* reviewer, is interesting. Hill commends the novel, observing that it "has a plausibility that suggests a closer view of the real facts."[7] That the novel "has a plausibility" is attested to by the many persons who, after reading the novel, asked Bates how often he had traveled in the South of France, the novel's setting, and by the readers who, upon seeing the author for the first time, gaped in surprise to find that he possessed both arms (the protagonist is an amputee). But Hill is mistaken when he concludes that this plausibility implies a "closer view of the real facts." The bare outline of the novel had been suggested to Bates in a brief conversation with a pilot who had been shot down over France

and escaped by a circuitous route. Beyond that skeleton of fact, com-
bined with some study of maps and atlases, Bates's creation was imagina-
tive. He had never been to the South of France and of course was not an
amputee.

Bates's reliance on creating through imagination rather than re-
creating through observation and experience is not forced by circumstance but is an aesthetic choice. Fiction, avows Bates, is an art of
"lying and distortion."[8] Throughout his career Bates had based his
novels and stories on a sudden glimpse of a passerby, a half-remembered
tale told by a relative, "those stray crumbs of gossip which are so often
enough to set the imagination of writers on fire" (*World in Ripeness*, 26).
In this regard, his fiction comes closer to that of Henry James—whose
work, ironically, Bates detested—than to such contemporaries as Joyce,
Hemingway, and Wolfe: all fond of transposing fact into fiction, often
with only the barest alteration.

Fair Stood the Wind for France concerns a downed English bomber
pilot's adventures in occupied France: his loss of an arm, his growing
love for a brave French girl, their desperate flight through dangerous,
degenerate Vichy France, their eventual escape into neutral Spain.
Seemingly such a departure from the earlier novels of rural life in the
English Midlands, *Fair Stood the Wind for France* bears the same economic, descriptive style, the same effective if not profound characterization,
the same indirection and understatement to heighten tension.

For instance, the novel is narrated through the point of view of
Franklin, the pilot, until the morning when he is to have his arm
amputated by two doctors. Then, however, the focus shifts to Françoise,
the French girl, who idly fishes in a calm little river, seemingly at peace
with the world, until she tears a fish-hook from the fish's mouth: "And
in that moment, as the hook tore the flesh of the fish and the blood
opened scarlet on her brown hands in the twilight, she knew for the first
time what they were going to do to Franklin."[9] The scene climaxes when
Françoise returns to the house at the moment that the doctor descends
the stairs carrying in a bloody towel "something" which he plops down
on the table, then proceeds to wash his hands, mixing Franklin's blood
with the blood of the fish. The scene closes as he remarks, matter-of-
factly, "Good fish" (118). It is a fine scene, muted and understated,
somehow more horrible in its surface serenity than any gory, direct
description of the butchery could possibly have been.

Scenes such as Franklin's amputation and the equally understated but
brutal scene of Françoise's father's suicide save the novel from being the
sentimental, melodramatic romance which a bare outline of the plot

might suggest. Bates's skillful characterization of Franklin also elevates the novel above the tired Hollywood "grade B" romance of the strong, silent warrior escaping into the sunset with his love. Little, Brown's flap copy on the jacket of their 1944 edition of the novel describes a pilot's "gentle strength, his sensitive mind, the carefully restrained warmth of his emotion" but surely this describes anyone other than Franklin, who is alternately jealous, destructively prideful, self-interested, often stupid. At one point he himself realizes that he is a "blind, impatient, and utterly selfish fool" (197). Time and again he is saved from doom only by luck and the tireless courage and sustaining faith of Françoise.

Paradoxically, even though the lovers do escape, the tone of the novel is hardly affirmative or triumphant. The dominant tone is one of impending doom: "an air of fatalism" (*World in Ripeness*, 23) as Bates called it. In most lesser romantic "escape" novels we are shocked if the lovers do not succeed; here we are surprised when they do. The most lasting impression from the novel is not the triumph of Franklin and Françoise, but the suffocating air of degeneracy enveloping Vichy France; its corruption, its cowardice, its surrender before battle. It is not coincidental that the title of the novel is taken from the first line of a Michael Drayton poem, "Agincourt," celebrating the English defeat of the French. In fact and in spirit, Vichy France is the enemy in the novel, not the Germans.

If Vichy France is the negative in the novel, the positive is no single character or nation, but youth itself: "the world of being young on the edge of danger, the experience of running your finger along the thread holding things together and not knowing if or how soon the thread would break" (85). Bates "saw the entire story as one epitomising the youth of two countries, on the one hand England almost alone in the battle, on the other France alone in humiliation and defeat" (*World in Ripeness*, 237). Franklin recognized in Françoise an "immense assurance, frightening because it was so clear and unequivocal and young" (53). If Franklin does not sense the same thing in himself, the reader does, and it is this indomitable spirit of youth which saves him from his many faults. Youth is the corollary of Vichy France's toothless cowardice. When France encounters danger, she capitulates; when youth encounters danger, it recognizes "the tenseness, the silence, the beauty of the moment" (206). That the two lovers are young and can recognize the beauty of a danger and tragedy that heightens life explains the enigmatic last line of the novel. Having just escaped France—Françoise's father a suicide, Franklin's best friend gunned down at the border—Franklin sees Françoise weeping, and ". . . there came tears in his own eyes,

and because of his tears, the mountains were dazzling in the sun"
(270).

Beauty and tragedy, triumph and death, youth and degeneracy: *Fair Stood the Wind for France* contains the fusion of the negative and the positive which Bates felt to be essential for the novel. He had ranged beyond the Midlands with great success, a success he would repeat in the novel, with an ever-expanding audience, throughout the remainder of the 1940s.

Chapter Five

The Fruits of Success (1946-50)

Although the Flying Officer 'X' stories and *Fair Stood the Wind for France* brought their author little immediate financial reward, they did make Bates's name known to a far wider audience than he had enjoyed prior to World War II. Financial success was reserved for the years immediately following the war, when Bates drew upon the material he had gathered while "eavesdropping" as Flying Officer 'X'—anecdotes, bits of conversation, random sensory impressions—to compose a series of novels set in the Far East: *The Purple Plain* (1947), *The Jacaranda Tree* (1949), and *The Scarlet Sword* (1950). All three were even more popular than *Fair Stood the Wind for France*; and since Bates did once again collect royalties from their sales (which to his chagrin he did not for *Fair Stood the Wind for France*), he was quite comfortable financially from that time on.

As is often the case, critical acclaim did not always accompany the financial success of the novels. A short novel—more properly termed a novella,[1] perhaps—published just after the close of the war received a far better reception from critics.

The Cruise of the Breadwinner (1946)

By 1946 Bates was already a veteran of writing about men at war. Even though *The Cruise of the Breadwinner* is another story about World War II, however, it marks something of a departure, and perhaps something of a risk, for Bates. Bates had gleaned a wealth of observations and experiences as Flying Officer 'X,' and he had an established, enthusiastic audience for works drawing upon those experiences. But *The Cruise of the Breadwinner* does not heavily draw upon those experiences, although it does involve a downed R.A.F. flyer; it is a work almost entirely of imagination. Another element of risk was the timing of the book. The Flying Officer 'X' stories were published at a time when all Englishmen's thoughts were filled with the war; England needed and appreciated stories showing the dauntless courage of her young warriors. But by 1946 England was adamantly and defiantly tired of the war. Could another war novel find a receptive audience? *The Cruise of the Breadwinner* proved that it could; and Bates—and many other novelists such as Nicholas Monsarrat (*The Cruel Sea*, 1951) and Charles Morgan (*The River Line*, 1949)—continued throughout the 1940s and early 1950s to write commercially successful novels set during World War II, although none of the English literature of the Second World War approached the tragic brilliance of the World War I poets and novelists.

The Cruise of the Breadwinner is more than simply an analysis of the horrors of war. In his introduction to *Six Stories*, Bates compares his novella to its thematic predecessor, *The Red Badge of Courage*, in that both involve a naive youth who confronts war in its bloody, palpable horror and returns "strangely grown in stature and refined by fire."[2] Thus, *The Cruise of the Breadwinner* is more than an account of a harrowing incident of war; it is a fictional *rite de passage*, a dramatization of a boy's psychic journey from youth to maturity.

The boy, Snowy, works aboard *The Breadwinner*—a small fishing vessel converted to a patrol craft—with the captain, Gregson, and the cynical engineer, Jimmy. All patrols to date had been uneventful affairs, and Snowy yearns to witness some exciting event from the war: ". . . the sea rescue of a pilot, the wreck of a plane, or even the firing of the Lewis gun. He had longed for all these things to happen on all patrols of *The Breadwinner* with a bright and narrow desire that kept him awake at night."[3]

Snowy gets his wish when they hear an aerial battle out to sea and sail off in search of possible downed pilots. Soon they rescue an English pilot swimming in the sea, and then his adversary, a German. Both are wounded, both colorful, and Snowy ached "to be part of the world of men" (42). Below deck making tea for the pilots and crew, Snowy hears running on deck. "He had at that moment reached the fine and rapid conclusion that war was wonderful" (43). But war turns from wonderful to hideous when he hears machine-gun fire bursting out above him, ascends to the decks and sees the results of a strafing attack: Jimmy blown to bits beside the Lewis gun and Gregson and the two pilots in a bloody heap. Gregson, miraculously, is unharmed, but the pilots' fresh wounds will soon prove fatal.

The remainder of the story concerns Gregson and Snowy's efforts to comfort the dying pilots and get the disabled *Breadwinner* back to shore. Snowy pities the English pilot and vascillates between grudging admiration and bitter hatred for the German. Snowy's attitude remains naive; his is still a world of heroes and villains, with all the horrors of war conveniently blamed on the Germans. But near the end when the boat finally approaches shore, Gregson bursts out in a tirade against "all the bastards, all over the world" (111), and this seems to crystallize the issue for Snowy. War is no longer a glamorous affair with heroes and villains; war and its universal suffering are the villains. At the end we are left with Snowy's implicit realization of the emotional distance he has traveled in one short afternoon: "He had been out with men to War and had seen the dead. He was alive and *The Breadwinner* had come home" (112).

In contrast to the majority of Bates's previous works, in *The Cruise of the Breadwinner* plot and characterization are more important than atmosphere. Equally interesting and important to the theme is a "sight pattern" of sorts—a motif incorporating images, items, references, and actions suggesting sight, vision, blindness, similar to the one found in *King Lear*—which parallels Snowy's maturation process.

For instance, the one thing for which Snowy yearns above all else is a pair of binoculars—the better to see the glamorous events of the war, of course. Gregson had promised him a pair long ago but not delivered, and Snowy covets those worn by the German pilot. What Snowy in fact needs is vision, maturity of vision. Ironically, he is noted for his ability to identify aircraft at great distances, even by their sound; but significantly, the one time that his talent is put to the test, he fails. "Spit pilot?" he asks the English pilot. "Typhoon," he is corrected (28). Thus, the binoculars underscore his need not only for sight, but insight into the true nature of war, suffering, death.

But the "sight pattern'" involves much more than simply the symbolic binoculars. Almost all suggestions of maturity or immaturity, ignorance or experience, are couched in terms of vision or blindness. Thus, when Snowy hears the machine-gun fire and rushes up to the deck—just after reaching the "fine and rapid conclusion that war was wonderful" (43)—"he became for some seconds quite sightless, as if he had stared at the sun" (46). He is numbed by what he sees. The air feels suddenly cold, "then still colder on his eyes, shocked stiff by what he had seen of the engineer" (47). He runs off "like a blind man. . . . He had seen the dead" (48).

Snowy's flight away from Jimmy carries him only to another horrifying sight, the two pilots gravely wounded, but he helps Gregson get them below deck, and his maturation process begins quickly. He passes Jimmy's corpse again, but "He was no longer aware of the shock of seeing blood for a second time. He was elevated into a world of catastrophe and pain . . ."(68). Appropriately, when he finally does take up the German's prized binoculars after the strafing attack, "What he saw through the grey and misty glasses was only a world of unproportioned light. It had no relation to the things he expected" (71). At this point Snowy's immature vision has been dispelled, only to be replaced by blindness and confusion, certainly not maturity. He begins, however, to take tentative steps toward a more balanced, mature vision. He still distrusts the German, but when he sees the two pilots lying in quiet pain below deck, "there did not seem to be very much difference between the appearance of the two men lying on the floor" (87). After they die, "now the lamplight was full on both of them, with equal brightness, as they lay side by side" (105).

Here Snowy is being offered that balanced vision, if only he will accept it; but the Englishman's death plunges him into another fog of blind hatred against the German pilot and Germany. Indeed, as they near the shore and safety, they are bound in a deep fog, which begins to lift when Gregson bursts out in bitter invective against "all the bastards, all over the world" (111).

This seems to be the grain that tips the balance. Snowy suddenly loses all desire to look through the binoculars. He can "see" now, after all. He thinks again of the two pilots, "And they became for him, at that moment, all the pilots, all the dead pilots, all over the world" (112). The end underscores his maturing vision in a sight image: "He had been out with men to war and had *seen* [italics mine] the dead. He was alive and *The Breadwinner* had come home" (112).

Three Novels of the Far East

The Cruise of the Breadwinner was a popular success because it was an exciting story, trim and direct, with sympathetic characters; it was a critical success for the same reasons, in addition to having an important theme and characters not only sympathetic but human enough to engage us in their psychological as well as physical conflict. Bates followed this success with three novels in four years set in the Far East, all based, at least in part, on Bates's observations while serving with the Air Ministry in India and Burma. The three far exceeded *The Cruise of the Breadwinner*'s popular success but fell short of its critical acclaim. In his autobiography Bates frequently refers to certain friends' growing distress at the direction his writing was taking in these novels. He implies that their objections centered primarily on his abandoning the novels of Midland life for more exotic locales; and his defense was that he wrote out of almost a compulsion, not a desire, that the novels were a sort of catharsis for "the powerful and almost catastrophic impact the East had on my sensitivity."[4]

If his friends' distress was based merely on a change of settings, critical disenchantment reflects a more fundamental shift in Bates's aesthetic priorities. The novels are not crashing failures, certainly, but each is flawed, each succeeding one more so than its predecessor. All have too much the flavor of the "best-seller" about them, exploiting sex and violence, telling little about the essential nature or effect of either, while too often neglecting the aesthetic verity of the novel: a proper integration of plot, characterization, and theme.

Of the three, *The Purple Plain* (1947) most nearly rises above the "best-seller" tag. The protagonist's conflict is engaging, the setting hypnotically painted, and the plot is frequently exciting. Equally important, Bates weaves a rich tapestry of imagery that underscores plot, theme, and characterization.

The protagonist is Forrester, an R.A.F. flight commander at an isolated airstrip bordering the scalding plain (the purple plain) of Burma. The germ for Forrester's inner conflict came to Bates on the very day of his demobilization. A fellow officer remarked upon a pilot who had gotten to be a much-decorated hero by the dubious method of trying to get himself killed. It happened that his wife had been blown out of his arms and killed by a German bomb while they were dancing on their honeymoon. Thereafter, he went into the air hoping to be killed, only to down plane after German plane instead (*Blossoming World*, 108). Bates appropriated this dilemma for his suicidal hero, Forrester, in whom subordinates and fellow officers see clearly "the signs of fiber disintegration, the moral breakup, the end."[5]

Almost unbeknown to Forrester, however, some genuine feeling for life still stirs him occasionally. He craves solitude yet still feels stabs of pity for his detestable tent-mate, Blore. He is contemptuous of his own life yet is stunned by the fiery death of a fellow pilot. He longs for death with each flight yet subconsciously scans the terrain below for avenues of escape in the event of a crash. The commingling of Forrester's death wish and life urge is reflected in the war, of course, but also in the dual nature of Burma itself: overabundant with life yet permeated with cruelty and death. The dualism of the Far East is captured in the opening image of the novel, where "flocks of small banana-green parrots" play in a "bombed pagoda" (3). Later, Forrester watches in horrified fascination as a tiny, innocent Burmese girl plays "an absorbing game of torment" (15) with a lizard until she kills it. And night after night, the lovely calm of the evening is fretted by jackals, "howling and crying like stricken voices in the hot darkness, almost without rest" (43). Finally, Burma's three-year drought reflects Forrester's spiritual drought, yet Burma has a saving grace: its people, represented by Anna, who helps rescue Forrester from his spiritual wasteland.

Anna is an educated young Burmese woman who, along with a very few others, survived a long trek from Rangoon to escape the advancing Japanese. She survived terrible hardships while watching most of her companions die, so like Forrester she is an intimate of life's horrors. Yet she has achieved a serenity and implicit balanced view of life that allows her to enjoy the beauty that life offers while recognizing and fighting against its depredations. Her alliance with the more fertile side of nature is signified by the pale green dress that she wears and the frangipani flower (its blossoms last forever, seemingly) caught in her hair.

Almost immediately upon their first meeting Forrester is captivated by Anna's beauty and even more by her wise, earned serenity. He leaves that first meeting terrified by his previous desire for death, and when he sees a fellow pilot die in a plane crash the next day, he realizes how very much he wants to live. His newfound desire for life is put to the test when he, the detested Blore, and the young navigator Carrington crash-land in the middle of the blistering hot wasteland that is the Burmese plain. Resting by day and walking by night, with no food and only a little water, Forrester survives the heat and the madness of Blore, who eventually kills himself, to literally carry the injured Carrington on his back to rescue. Thus, Forrester's march to survival mirrors Anna's earlier one, and in the process he has earned a portion of her serenity: even at the bleakest hour on the plain, he thinks of Anna and is struck by the "essential and terrific wonder of things" (242).

Structurally, *The Purple Plain* breaks into two distinct halves: the first half at the airstrip and nearby village where Anna lives and the second half on the plain. To say that the two halves do not fit together is not entirely accurate; we have already shown that the struggle on the plain, carrying Carrington "piggyback," tests Forrester's desire to live and his commitment to his fellow man. Yet nagging problems remain for the reader. Forrester's spiritual demon is his desire for death, yet for all practical purposes that demon is exorcised in his first visit to Anna in the second chapter. His aching hollowness at the loss of his wife is assuaged in the sixth chapter, only a third of the way through the novel, when he holds Anna in his arms during a bombing attack. This scene mirrors the one in which Forrester lost his wife, so we know that he has found a replacement.

Thus the novel ends, thematically, before it is half over. At no time in his struggles on the plain do we doubt Forrester's will to live or his desire to get back to Anna. We gain no new insight about him as a man or about man's condition in a world rich in life and death. Bates's account of the trek across the plain is a masterful *tour de force* of action and description—the equal of any in Bates's long career—and it is worth reading for that alone; yet it would be just as satisfying had it been published alone as a novella, apart from the story of Anna.

Instead, the affair of Forrester and Anna forces Bates into an ending more reminiscent of popular Hollywood movies (and *The Purple Plain* was filmed as a movie starring Gregory Peck) than the intelligent and ruthlessly realistic novels and stories upon which his reputation was founded. After Forrester and Carrington are rescued and properly treated, Forrester returns to the little Burmese village where Anna lives. But his friend Harris, who introduced him to Anna, is ominously silent during the jeep ride to the village; he avoids answering questions and does not laugh at Forrester's jokes. In the village, the people shrink back with averted eyes before Forrester. Anna is not with the others, and a friend refuses to answer when Forrester asks where she is. We have been given all the traditional signs that Anna is dead, obviously, yet Forrester finds that she is merely asleep. He lies down beside her, and the novel ends.

Bates has shamelessly and pointlessly manipulated our feelings at the end; there simply is no reason for Harris's silence, the averted eyes, the unwillingness to answer a simple question. And there is other evidence that Bates could not decide between a serious book with a powerful theme and a "best-seller." It is a little too facile, for instance, that a bombing raid forces Anna into Forrester's arms for that first kiss, just as previously a bombing raid forced his wife out of his arms before their marriage could be consummated. And perhaps we have cause to complain when the only major character who does not survive is the one who, after all, is not very likable and so little loss: Blore. Most disturbing is the realization that all the characters save Forrester are one-dimensional types: not the colorful and interesting types that evolved from characters that Bates grew up with in his Midland youth, but types that we have seen and expect to see in movies and "best-sellers."

If we wonder whether at this point in his career Bates was teetering on the edge between serious fiction and more purely popular fiction, a look at his next two novels of the Far East will not be very encouraging.

The Jacaranda Tree (1949) was even more popular than *The Purple Plain* and presents even more problems for the discriminating reader. A brief summary of the plot seems to indicate a novel that could not help but be diverting, even exciting. Peterson is the English manager of a mill in a small Burmese town when news comes that a Japanese advance is imminent. Peterson organizes the British inhabitants of the village, together with his Burmese mistress and her brother, for what he hopes will be an orderly evacuation to India. Included in the group are a young Englishwoman who has been "jilted" by Peterson; his petty and envious assistant manager, Portman; Portman's snobbish but beautiful wife, who tries to seduce Peterson; a loud and bigoted Englishman, Betteson, who verbally and physically brutalizes his scatter-brained but compassionate wife; and so on. Peterson is forced to try to move this largely uncooperative group up the length of Burma, through hordes of panicked Burmese, with the Japanese in hot pursuit. How can the novel be anything other than exciting?

To be fair, the novel is exciting in places, and Bates's well-established descriptive powers occasionally enthrall us, although never with the force seen in the last half of *The Purple Plain*. The problems with *The Jacaranda Tree* are twofold: tone and characterization. The novel is peopled for the most part with characters who are dangerously oblivious to the enormous changes taking place in their world. Vestiges of the British Empire, they can hardly comprehend the imminent danger of the Japanese invasion, much less the more sweeping currents that are rapidly washing away the remains of the empire. Betteson is a choleric old worker in a steamship office who is obsessed with the "tricky issues" that upset his life; war for him is simply another of these "tricky issues." Portman is far more interested in reliving his days in India as a member of the Bengal Club than in being a productive worker at the mill, and his wife is supremely irritated that the war will interfere with her gossiping and showing off her "perfect" body evenings at the Swimming Club. Mrs. McNairn insists on being late for Peterson's meeting to plan the evacuation because "It was exceedingly bad to be early; it lowered you in people's eyes."[6]

Indeed, the first third of *The Jacaranda Tree* has more nearly the flavor of an English comedy of manners moved to Burma than a serious study of civilians caught up in the horrors of war, and it is here that the novel is most original and interesting. It is when the tone changes to what we expected all along that we begin to lose interest. Knowing Bates's considerable skills, we would expect the novel to have great power and suspense once the action shifts to the long flight up the road to India, but too often it does not. The cause of the flight, the Japanese, never appear in more than rumor; and the rumors hardly stir the characters, much less the reader. Mrs. Portman's frequent attempts to seduce Peterson are only half-hearted, she being no more than mildly interested in the whole affair, Peterson and the reader not at all. Nothing whatsoever comes of the potential racial issue; Nadia, Peterson's Burmese mistress, is a faultless young goddess, and the comic outrage of the bigots leads nowhere in the action or theme. In the end, every character whom Bates has caused us to dislike gets killed off—every single one—and each character with whom we sympathize, save one, survives. Peterson, Nadia, and her brother are saved in Hollywood fashion. The cavalry comes to the rescue, in this case the cavalry represented by a British convoy.

The novel might still have been saved from its inconsistency of tone and flaws in the dramatic action if we were presented with one strong character to build an engaging theme and conflict around, but unfortunately we are not. Peterson, the protagonist, is largely a mystery, and a confusing, not an engaging, mystery. Bates presents Peterson in the first chapter as an irritable man, frequently drunk. His servant-boy, Tuesday, gauges his moods by the number of aspirin he demands each morning; and while Tuesday worships his master, he also stands poised to dodge in case Peterson slings a glass or bottle at him: evidently a common practice. What is the cause of Peterson's unhappiness, irritation, dipsomania, or whatever it is? We never know.

Peterson's predecessor as mill manager had surrounded his house with a beautiful garden, but Bates emphasizes in the opening pages that Peterson "did not seem to care for gardens, and nothing remained of it" (4) except a single jacaranda tree. If there has been one phenomenon that we can count on in Bates's fiction, it is that a person who has a healthy relationship to and love for nature will be a positive character, and those who do not, will not. All the early indications, then, lead us to believe that Peterson has some basic problem or flaw, but the opposite is the case. In the remainder of the novel he proves to be a likable enough fellow, competent, rational, even tempered. He is well liked by the Burmese, and he returns their affection; if his relationship with the rest of the Britishers is less happy, in every case it is their fault, not his. Indeed, other than the task of leading his little group out of danger, he has no conflict, no problem. He learns nothing essential about himself, about Burma, about life in general during the course of his struggle because he apparently had no questions in the first place.

About the only question that the reader has is how soon will the bad fellows (Portman, Betteson, Mrs. McNairn) get their due, and how much trouble will they cause the good fellows before that happens. In other words, in *The Jacaranda Tree* Bates comes closer than ever before to the facile conflicts and resolutions of the best-seller.

In some ways, the last novel of Bates's Far East trilogy, *The Scarlet Sword* (1950), is the most satisfying of the three, in some ways the least. The story of an English mission in Kashmir pillaged during the bloody days of the Indian partition, *The Scarlet Sword* avoids both the flawed thematic structure of *The Purple Plain* and the inconsistency of tone and characterization of *The Jacaranda Tree*; and it very nearly avoids the sentimentalism that caused Bates to kill off the unpleasant characters and save the likable ones in both. Indeed, the violence and horror in and about the mission strike the innocent and guilty, the holy and unholy alike (although early on we do sense quite correctly that the violence will spare the protagonist, his new love, a likable priest, and a courageous nurse).

The virtue of *The Scarlet Sword* is its single-mindedness. It evokes the violent world of rape, murder, and torture that marked the India partition with a relentlessness that forces the reader to keep turning the pages. But if this single-mindedness allows Bates to avoid the pitfalls of structure and tone that flawed the previous two novels of the Far East, it also prevents him from engaging us on any other level. We might have been even more captivated by the action, for example, if we were a little engaged by the characters, but Bates gives us too little to go on. We know next to nothing about Crane, the protagonist. In reply to a question about his religion, he says, "I'm not anything."[7] When asked where he is from, he shrugs, "I'm not from anywhere" (39). All we know is that he is a reporter, rather tired, rather cynical, little more than a shadowy version of Forrester from *The Purple Plain*. And Bates gives us no reason to disbelieve Crane's first impression of Julie Maxted, with whom he will later fall in love: "She was another one who had flounced her way through the war with no other wounds but the sores on her finger tips from tying Red Cross parcels" (41).

The Scarlet Sword opens with a host of characters—tired, cynical, and frightened—and closes with a much-reduced host, laughing. We can only guess why they are tired and cynical in the beginning or why they are laughing at the end: unless it is that it is very nice to be alive when one might have been dead, and that is hardly revelation enough to build a novel around.

Bates had spent two decades building a reputation as a writer who could skillfully and engagingly weave stories and novels that told us a good deal about individuals, specific segments of society, specific epochs of history, and the human condition. With the three novels of the Far East, he seems to be attempting the same thing in an altered setting; but for all their sweeping action, varied characters, colorful and exotic settings, we do not learn much about men or man, place or time in the three novels. We are left primarily with violent action and love affairs, the stuff of best-sellers. We can easily see why Bates was reaching an ever-expanding audience, while at the same time leaving behind old friends who longed for him to return to the settings and characters of the Midlands.

Dear Life (1949)

Although it has been useful for us to discuss the three novels of the Far East as a group, they were not published consecutively. Their writing and publication order was interrupted by a strange little novel, *Dear Life*, which was published before *The Scarlet Sword* in the same year, 1949, as *The Jacaranda Tree*.

Bates hardly mentions *Dear Life* in his autobiography. Critical reaction was almost universally adverse. Its "forgotten child" status is underscored by the fact that later publishers, if they acknowledge it at all, include it under short stories in their lists of Bates's publications. It should not simply be dismissed as a forgettable failure, however. Rather, if any work in Bates's long career deserves reconsideration, it is *Dear Life*.

Dear Life is the powerfully bleak portrait of a teenage girl living in the nightmarish physical and spiritual wasteland of post–World War II London. Laura lives in a dismal basement flat with her vulgar mother, abusive stepfather, Oakley, and her unbalanced Uncle "Cupid," who spends his days in silence, hoarding money under his bed and furiously knitting away at tangles of scarlet wool. Having lost the emotional center of her life, her father, in a bombing raid during the war, Laura craves any sort of gentleness or affection. She does not find it from her mother or stepfather, both of whom bully her into turning down the offer of a scholarship so that she can work; therefore, she turns to Johnny. But Johnny is a small-time hoodlum, and when he is caught by the police, "there was an end of the gentleness in Johnny; the feeling, discovered among rubble and seeded buddleia trees of blitzed places down the street, of being wanted and being understood. There was an end of lying down together behind the old air-raid shelters, in places where unluckier people had died, and hungrily making love, cruelly clinging to every second that kept her away from the bed on the floor of the basement room and the frenzied scarlet entanglement of Uncle Cupid fighting with his nerves."[8]

Laura's London is a wasteland of easy sex, easier violence, bomb craters and blasted buildings, a place where shadowy foreigners are as common as Englishmen, a place where inhabitants stumble as if in shock, remnants of a ruined civilization. One possible avenue of escape for Laura is a job. She is given a position in the office of births and deaths. It has two filing cabinets, jokes her boss, Steerson: "Bodies in one. Babies in the other. . . . Level each other out in time" (35). Steerson is a scatterbrain who makes numerous promises but immediately forgets them, asks numerous solicitous questions without bothering to wait for an answer. Before Laura can consider whether her job is more tolerable than her basement room, she meets Clay, an ex-soldier from Canada. In a furious rampage out of London across the countryside, she accompanies Clay on a spree of mindless robbery and murder, until Clay is gunned down and Laura captured. The novel ends without a hint of resolution, condemnation, or hope.

We know from the novels of the Far East, as well as earlier novels and stories, that violence is nothing new to Bates's fictive world. Neither the fact nor the quantity of violence in *Dear Life* shocks us so much as its nature, mindless and unrepentant, and the method which Bates employs to present a bleak fable of a world in ruin.

Several scenes show Bates's skill in creating a world so grotesquely soulless and violent as to transcend the real to the surreal. One of the strangest, if not the most violent, is Laura's first meeting with Clay. Laura walks down a windy, deserted street and releases a brown paper bag, which blows against the legs of a man who is suddenly, with "terrifying silence" (27) simply "there." The man is Clay, with the cold and ominous aura of death that his name implies, and he talks to Laura a few minutes before she hurries off. After a long walk down winding streets, Laura loses her hat in the black, oily river, and suddenly Clay is "there" again, appearing with a silent suddenness of a specter. He offers to retrieve her hat, then disappears into the shadow of the bridge. Laura hears a splash and waits over ten minutes, but there is no sign of Clay. She goes home. The scene ends without hint of explanation, lending an intensely eerie mood to the novel.

Like a bad penny, Clay shows up days later. He exhibits occasional flashes of tenderness and affection for Laura, but she is most impressed by his promise to "knock Oakley to hell" (76). This he does: coldly, methodically, murderously. Oakley dead, they steal a car and flee

London for the countryside, where one of the most surreal episodes occurs: the robbery of a toy shop.

They believe the toy shop to be deserted, and as they search, a cupboard door "came flying open like the lid of a jack-in-the-box, exploding pyramids of colored hats" (107). Instead of money they find an old lady. Laura holds a gun on the woman while Clay searches the rest of the shop. Laura senses someone behind her and turns to see another old lady with a "bright green fire engine" raised over her head; she throws it and it lands in the middle of the room "with exactly the effect of an exploding bomb" (113). But the explosion is actually Laura's gun going off as she shoots the first woman; Clay rushes back in and "takes care of" the second. For a few moments after her first murder, Laura stands stunned by fear, clutching a doll, but then she shakes off the fear in a shrug of contempt. The chapter ends with Clay's words of praise: "You're a great kid" (116).

She is a "kid," of course, as is emphasized by the doll she clutches and the toy-shop setting of her murder. She is but one of a generation of English youth bequeathed a heritage of ruin, a generation whose memories are of war (the "bomb" exploding in the middle of the room) and who grow into the violent fruit of the blasted soil that nurtured them. They will become the "Teddy boys" of the 1950s. The scenes cited above are but two in a novel filled with horror. Laura is so steeped in horror that when Clay is gunned down on the stairs of a deserted mansion, itself a bombed-out relic of the war, Laura walks out on the same stairs, gazes down at his riddled body, and blithely arranges a hair grip before going out to meet her captors. As she marches on down the stairs, her last thoughts are of Uncle Cupid "knitting for his nerves, knitting for dear life" (149).

Dear Life is a trim, tightly woven novel, pared down to the essentials. The imagery—the gory scarlets and crimsons that splash Bates's canvas, the pigeon that "carved the spring sky like a grey sickle" (55)—support the violent characters, action, and theme. It is not a pleasant novel to read—its virtuosity is a painful one—and that perhaps contributed to its poor critical reception. In many ways it is a novel ahead of its time; no such savage vision of postwar English youth will be seen until Golding's *Lord of the Flies* and Burgess's *A Clockwork Orange*, and both of those present possible worlds rather than the horribly actual world of *Dear Life*. As an indictment of soulless postwar English society it is infinitely more powerful and honest than the "angry young man" fiction that followed in the 1950s (to be discussed in Chapter 7). It reminds us of nothing so much as the news accounts of the disaffected youth in the

United States in the 1950s (such as Charles Starkweather's murderous rampage across the Midwest with his teenage girl friend). It is a difficult novel to place in Bates's canon or in the tradition of the English novel up to 1950, yet—for that reason, perhaps—*Dear Life* richly deserves reevaluation.

Chapter Six

The Second Flowering: The Short Story in the Later Years (1951—74)

Although *The Cruise of the Breadwinner* and *Dear Life* were brilliantly achieved works, comparable to the best of Bates's career, certainly the most "visible" products of the years immediately following World War II were the three novels of the Far East: extremely popular money-makers all, but flawed works, as we have seen. The possibility that Bates's reputation might rest on these popular novels is lamentable. His fiction before World War II is far more interesting, original, and characteristic of his career in general than the popular novels; and although the fiction in the last two decades of his writing career is uneven in quality, he frequently approaches his high standards of the 1930s. As ever, in the later years of his career, Bates was astoundingly prolific; he published eight new collections of short stories (plus one published posthumously), eleven novels, five collections of novellas, and one novella published separately. Because of the large volume of material in the later years, we can most profitably discuss the three fiction genres separately: thus, we will devote one chapter each to the short story, the novel, and the novella in the later years.

Especially in the short story, the decades of the 1950s and 1960s represent something of a second flowering for Bates. Although the influence of the popular novel could be felt in all of Bates's fiction in the later years, the short-story form by its very nature could survive the thin characterization that scarred the novels of the Far East; and in the short story, the exotic locales, which Bates still occasionally used, added spice to, rather than smothered, the atmosphere. Finally, plot—by Bates's admission never a great interest or strength[1]—rarely assumes a dominant role in the short story as it often did in the popular novels, to their detriment.

The short stories in the 1950s and 1960s mark a return both to the high standards and the methods of the prewar years. Indeed, *Colonel Julian and Other Stories* (1951), *The Daffodil Sky* (1955), and *The Enchantress and Other Stories* (1961) warrant comparison with Bates's finest collections; and *The Watercress Girl and Other Stories* (1959)—Bates's unique collection representing the fruition of his interest in the world of the young—is as consistently praised by reviewers as any of his efforts.

Colonel Julian and Other Stories (1951)

The selections in *Colonel Julian and Other Stories* exemplify Bates's developing concerns in the later years while they at the same time employ many of the same methods and themes that served him for twenty-five years. Four of the stories are set in India, Burma, or the Continent, while only three—aside from the two new Uncle Silas stories—are set in the Midland countryside. The exotic settings, of course, result from Bates's interest in the war, and five of the stories deal in whole or in part with the effects of the war on the individual and society.

Granted that the war is the subject for over a third of the stories in the collection, however, it actually is only the most extreme manifestation of a theme that we witnessed with increasing frequency in the 1930s: the ravages of time and a changing culture. This is the primary or at least ancillary theme of two-thirds of the *Colonel Julian* stories. "A Girl Called Peter," for example, concerns an even older Bates theme: a girl whose romantic inclinations are warped by a repressive father. But the young man to whom Peter becomes attracted displays some of Bates's bitterness at the changing face of England. When Peter asks if someone will move into the old mansion that the young man is surveying, he answers, "It's much more likely that they'll pull it down. Bong goes another bit of England."[2]

War's role in the acceleration of cultural change is seen in purest terms in the title story, "Colonel Julian." The colonel is an eighty-three-year-old veteran of the wars in India whose mansion is being used to billet flyers during World War II. Colonel Julian loves to talk to the flyers about their exploits, although their R.A.F. slang makes their speech nearly incomprehensible to him. Even this is cultural change, of course: "Language in his day had been rather a pompous affair, perhaps rather puerile, but he felt that at least you could understand it. He did not understand this other at all. He felt sometimes like a young boy left out in the cold, not yet initiated into the secret of the games of older boys" (43). Too, in his day soldiers were soldiers, rugged and martial. But the modern flyers had a "touch of almost feminine dreaminess" (44) about them, along with an indefinable remoteness, cynicism. "There was none of that heroic stuff at all" (44).

The colonel is particularly interested in Mr. Pallister, a young flyer who has returned from horrible burns to "kill Huns" with a barracuda-like single-mindedness. The story ends with the news that Pallister "bought it" on his last flight over France. If Colonel Julian again fails to understand the language, we infer that he is suddenly confronted with the realization that war has changed from a heroic, romantic endeavor to some cold, unblinking thing that kills young boys indifferently and leaves the living little more than physical and emotional scar tissue.

Add to the interrelated themes of war and the ravages of time and cultural change a third, one that appears again and again in the stories: the failure of love and sex to compensate adequately for life's miseries. In fully two-thirds of the stories the protagonist attempts through love or sex to carve out an emotional haven but in the end finds himself facing a world of suffering and loneliness. Two of the finest stories in the collection, "The Flag" and "The Frontier," combine the three dominant themes of war, change, and the failure of love with painful effectiveness.

"The Flag" is the story of a traveler, the narrator, who stops off for a brief tour of a decaying English country estate. He remains long enough to discover that the alcoholic owner, the Captain, is in at least as advanced a state of disrepair as his mansion, and we infer that the Captain's wife's chief pleasure is dallying with the handyman, Williams.

It may seem strange to include this depressing little tale among the war stories, but the classification is appropriate. The Captain himself traces the material decline of his estate to the destruction caused by billeting troops there during the war. The mansion and grounds were "all done by great chaps . . . creative chaps. It's only we of this genera-tion who are such absolute destructive clots" (133), he moans, under-scoring our second major theme: the ravages of time and cultural change.

If we take the Captain as emblematic of the English landed gentry who are being crucified—the mansion itself is built in the form of a cross—by shifting cultural and economic patterns, we must conclude that the gentry hasten their own destruction by their ineffectuality. The Captain sops up drink after drink, and Bates captures his degenerate condition in distasteful nature images: "His ears were like thickly veined purple cabbage leaves unfurling on either side of flabby swollen cheeks. His mouth, pink and flaccid, trembled sometimes like the underlip of a cow" (131). And although the Captain's wife has such scorn for his ineffectuality, she is scarcely in any better condition. She makes her entrance carrying lilies (traditional symbols for death), and her complexion is marked by a deep pallor. Her hands "were not unlike long blanched stalks of uprooted flowers themselves" (136). Her lips were like a "tight scarlet bud," but her pallor makes the Captain's "festering rosiness seem more florid than ever" (136).

That both the Captain and his wife are totally dependent on their handyman, Williams, further underscores the uselessness of the gentry in contemporary England. Williams's "dark brown hair that he had allowed to grow into a curly pad on his neck" and "stiff correct strength" (136) contrast markedly to the wan flaccidity of his "betters." Significantly, Williams had been growing flowers when he is called onto the scene by the Captain's wife.

The story reaches its climax when the Captain and the narrator climb to the top of the tower for an overview of the rundown estate and a closer look at the flag. It had seemed "dead" (132) early in the story, and we now learn that it is not a flag of heraldry as we had supposed, but is merely something that the Captain had found stuffed in an attic box. Thus, the flag is a perfect symbol for a gentry sapped of life and stripped of honor. At this point the narrator looks down and sees the Captain's wife and Williams down below in the greenhouse—"inside the winking scarlet roof of glass" (141). In case we had not guessed from earlier hints, the "winking scarlet" strongly implies the nature of their relationship.

It is all too much for the Captain. He weeps drunkenly, "Never knew it was going to pot. . . . Everything. The whole damn thing" (140). His home, his wife, his culture are slipping away from him, are in fact lost forever.

"The Flag" is the exploration of a situation rather than a structured sequence of events. It relies upon atmosphere, imagery, and characterization for its effect, and thus employs much the same methods as his stories written before World War II. "The Frontier" is much longer and more strongly plotted and thus is more representative of Bates's fiction in the later years.

Both "The Flag" and "The Frontier," however, explore the same basic themes: the effects of war, the ravages of cultural change, and, perhaps most important, the failure of love to be a saving grace against the aforementioned. "The Frontier" was inspired by Bates's visit to an English tea-grower's estate in India. But it was not the beauty of the countryside or the primitive innocence of the Indians that haunted Bates and provided the seed for the story: it was the "great loneliness . . . great emptiness"[3] of the Englishman's life.

Owen is the middle-aged English plantation owner in "The Frontier." He shares a train cabin with Blake, a cynical young English nurse, and is startled when she accepts his rather perfunctory offer to spend the weekend with him at his tea plantation. There his half-hearted attempts to seduce her fail because of her bored, intimidating sangfroid, the ill-timed visit of his blustery neighbor, McFarlane, but mostly his own despairing ineffectuality.

Owen has every right to despair. The movement toward independence is felt throughout India, and nationalism is rampant. "Quit India" signs greet him along the road to his plantation. The old order is obviously changing, but to Owen "it was a step backward: the birth of another nationalism, the creation of yet another frontier" (237). Unfortunately, Owen, the old order, no longer has the vigor to face and conquer another frontier: "As they drove on he felt overwhelmed by his own inadequacy. . . . War had come and swept disastrously across the East like an awful flood and left him as he was" (237).

It is the war, of course, that brings Blake to him, but what sort of woman is she? Tired, bored, cold, hardened by her experiences, she is as intimidating to Owen as the new order; indeed, she is the new order. His one real attempt at seduction, forestalled by his "withering shyness" (234), ends in pathetic courtesy: "I just wanted to say that it was sweet of you to come. . . . Awfully sweet, and I'm awfully grateful" (235).

But Blake, after all, did not come to Owen's estate to be seduced—no such romantic notions for the new order. She came to join in the hunt for a crazed Indian killer. Owen tries to dissuade her, but nothing she does makes sense to him. He takes her for a drive into the foothills, and she insists on a swim despite the dangerous currents. He sits and watches beside the river, his river. "He felt that it was his own river; that the water was from his own snows, and that the snows were from his own mountains. This was his country . . ." (228).

The next moment we learn the fate of this possessive old order. The Indian killer steps out of the jungle, aims his rifle, and shoots—not the audacious young woman—but Owen. He dies in dumb agony in Blake's arms. The story's last line—"Now only she herself remained" (240)—shows that a new frontier awaits the cold, callous products of war: unutterable loneliness.

The Daffodil Sky (1955)

The Daffodil Sky is Bates's crowning achievement in the later years. Nine of the stories are included in The Best of H. E. Bates (1963), by far the largest share claimed by any collection. Although every reader will quibble with some selections for and some omissions from *The Best of H. E. Bates*, the large number of selections from *The Daffodil Sky* attests to its overall excellence. Only *Something Short and Sweet* rivals it for consistent quality.

Although *The Daffodil Sky* employs many of the same themes, methods, and settings that we saw in *Colonel Julian*, its primary distinguishing feature is its rich variety of tones. From the curiously melancholy affirmation of "The Good Corn" to the undercurrents of incest and violence in "The Daffodil Sky," from the nearly farcical irony of "Country Society" to the quiet compassion and humor of "The Common Denominator," from the painful acidity of "Elaine" to the gentle wit of "Go Lovely Rose," *The Daffodil Sky* stands out from previous collections where Bates tended to deal primarily in the subtle shadings of pathos.

In many ways *The Daffodil Sky* seems a throwback of sorts to the manner of the early collections, although they were certainly more limited in setting and subject matter than the present volume. Admittedly, the major efforts, at least in length, of the collection—"The Daffodil Sky," "Across the Bay," "A Place in the Heart," and "The Evolution of Saxby"—in their assiduous analysis of dangerous passion, ineffectuality, and loneliness would rest more comfortably in *Colonel Julian* than in *Day's End*; and most reviewers tend to emphasize these. Many of the most memorable tales, however, are short vignettes, examinations of situations rather than sequences of events. In these, atmosphere and characterization are dominant, with plot only minimally important, thus resembling many of the fine tales from Bates's early years.

"Elaine" is a good example. The narrator sits opposite a young couple on a train and occasionally meets the young woman's eyes. She is pretty and vibrant, but her companion is waspish and petulant and brutally rebuffs her attempts at conversation. The Elaine of the title is not the young woman. An Elaine is mentioned in passing, and the name obviously touches on a raw nerve; but who she is and what she represents to the couple, we never learn. But this is perfectly in keeping with the story. The narrator never comprehends why this lovely girl would allow herself to be treated so shamelessly by the obnoxious little man. When they deboard the train, the man leaves her to struggle with a multitude of packages, but she coldly and almost angrily rejects the narrator's offer of assistance. The story ends with her hurrying off through the rain after her companion; and narrator and reader are none the wiser, except that we know that we have confronted one painful and degrading aspect of passion.

"The Maker of Coffins" is another tale simple almost to the point of severity, yet it possesses a lyric beauty reminiscent of "Harvest" from *Day's End*. The tale presents a Sunday evening like all other Sunday evenings in the lives of Luther, the coffin maker, and his mother. Every Sunday evening he plays tunes on his fiddle for her—especially "the old 'uns . . . they take a bit o' beatin'"[4]—and it is evident that this is all that she has to look forward to in life. As he plays, both think of the past and future, and both know that he will soon be making a coffin for her. But the thought is not tragic or despairing. Death is simply another phase of living in this unassuming tale that in a few brief pages encompasses the past and the future in a serene, elegiac examination of the present moment.

"The Treasure Game" is a fine little tale that concerns Mrs. Fairfax, a middle-aged mother of two "children," as she calls them—actually both girls are nearing twenty. The theme is typically Batesian. Mrs. Fairfax obviously hates growing older while life continues all around her, and her frustration manifests itself in irritation at her two vivacious daughters, who are described in budding flower imagery.

On this particular day her irritation is directed at the girls' noisy garden party. But her mood changes when one of the "boys" crawls through the garden (a tempting snake?) and grabs her foot as she swings in a hammock. The young man had been playing "treasure game"—a variation on the traditional scavenger hunt where all items (a buckle, a strap, something white, something silk) obviously could represent various stages in a woman's undress. After swinging and talking with the young man and growing more enamored by the moment, Mrs. Fairfax finally gives him her shoe and stocking (items he needed to complete his list) and sends him on his way. The end of the story finds Mrs. Fairfax "alone but no longer deserted" (130), running her naked foot through the grass, in touch with nature once more.

Several other stories in *The Daffodil Sky* follow Bates's tried and true method of simplicity with implication. Obviously, merely summarizing the tales is as great an injustice as reducing a lyric poem to a paraphrase. Only by reading them can one begin to understand their artistry. But these simple tales represent Bates's true strength as a fiction writer, and on them and others like them his reputation will eventually rest.

Sugar for the Horse (1957) and The Watercress Girl and Other Stories (1959)

In the late 1950s Bates offered his readers a respite from his mostly somber, often bitter stories of contemporary life with the publication of two collections in a lighter vein: *Sugar for the Horse* and *The Watercress Girl and Other Stories*.

Sugar for the Horse is Bates's second collection of Uncle Silas stories, and our discussion in Chapter 4 of the tendencies and techniques found in *My Uncle Silas* (1939) applies here also. Bates's tendency to set Uncle Silas in unholy war against the forces of inhibition and convention is if anything more pronounced in *Sugar for the Horse* than its predecessor. "Queenie White," for example, is an open attack on the institution of marriage. The beautiful Queenie is married to the miserly Charly, but Silas convinces her to run off on a sexual holiday. They remain two weeks, living off sex and Charly's money. This crass violation of society's taboos, and even a beating by Charly, does not dampen Silas's enthusiasm in the least: "Hang about Charly. Hang about the old tits a-gossipin'. Hang about whether she were a married woman. Hang about the consequences. . . . What the 'Anover are we 'ere for? Not to be maungy old narrer-gutses like Charly White, I tell you! We're dead a long time."[5] With only slight injustice to Bates's philosophy, then, we can summarize the bulk of it in Silas's simple maxim: "Mek the most on it while you can" (35).

As we might well have predicted, the chief object of Silas's scorn and frequent target of his wrath is the church and its representatives. The opening lines of "The Foxes" demonstrate how natural this scorn is to the narrator (and Bates): "My Uncle Silas, not unnaturally, and as might have been expected, had little use for the church" (50). The climax of Silas's war against the church comes in the collection's final tale, "The Fire-Eaters," where Silas and two friends worry the old town parson to his grave, then engage the conflict with the new parson by building a bonfire with his furniture, ravishing his maid, and burning him in effigy.

Lying, cheating, stealing, adultery, arson, drunken sprees—these are the materials of Silas's escapades. Whereas we would condemn these same things in other works, however, in the Silas stories they are effective methods of attacking the hypocritical world of inhibition and repression. We may shake our heads skeptically, with the narrator, at some of Silas's claims, but we know that he—unlike most of Bates's unhappy protagonists—has found the secret of life.

The Watercress Girl and Other Stories (1959) is Bates's paean to youth. Reviewers are unanimous in their praise of the collection, and few readers will fail to be touched and amused by the selections. The prevalent tone of the stories is nostalgia, nostalgia not for an irrevocable past but for a manner of reacting to the present. Our experience in reading these tales is not always joyous, as it is, for instance, in the Uncle Silas stories. True, the nostalgia is so sweet in some of the stories and the atmosphere so lushly painted—as in "The Watercress Girl" and "Great Uncle Crow"—that the sense of loss is overshadowed; but in others innocence and naiveté translate to ignorance and misapprehension, not bliss. A good example is "Let's Play Soldiers," in which a gang of young boys wage furious war against rival gangs, reflecting the graver war in the world at large. At the end the protagonist witnesses the grief of a woman who has just learned of the death of her son, and his dreams of military glory turn bitter. As in "Let's Play Soldiers," in many of the stories in this collection the adult world is a portentous, threatening backdrop for the childhood visions.

All the tales in *The Watercress Girl* employ a double narrative point of view, although very subtly at times. That is, in each we witness a certain situation through the eyes of a young person, but this youthful vision is in turn seen through a more mature perspective; we "look back" at youth: thus, the nostalgia. This double perspective is occasionally harmful, as in "The Poison Ladies," where the older narrator, and thus the reader, refuses to be anything more than amused at the boys' fear of the house of the "poison ladies." A few of the stories, also, are merely nostalgic, and therefore, once our appetite for that particular emotion is satisfied, we find nothing of particular interest in plot, characterization, or theme.

We might make this complaint after a cursory reading of "The Cowslip Field," too, but closer examination reveals that nostalgia is only one component of a story that skillfully combines characterization, atmosphere, and theme. The action is typically spare. A young boy gathers cowslips in a field with Pacey, a squat, ugly, dwarfish woman. He continually asks naive questions, naive not because the answer is so obvious but because an adult would realize that the answer is unknowable or painful. "Will I grow any bigger? . . . Well then, why won't you?"[6] Pacey returns appropriately frivolous answers. Their gathering finished, the boy whimsically asks Pacey to let her hair down. When she does, he sees her transformed into an object of beauty and crowns her with a cowslip necklace. Pacey swings him around in grateful joy, and the story ends.

"The Cowslip Field" seems to be a happy little tale about an incident in a boy's youth. Yet pathos is the primary result. Why? Obviously, Pacey is lovely only to the child; to the adult world she is grotesque. The fact that the boy's naiveté allows him to see past the ugly surface to the beauty of the essential woman only underscores the tragedy and unfairness of her position in life. Thus, we sense Pacey's pain at the boy's innocent question, "Have you a young man, Pacey?" We infer the true answer from her exaggerated response: "Oh! dozens . . . scores" (12). When the boy with naive mercilessness tries to force her to tell exactly when she will get married, she distracts him by urging him to complete his cowslip necklace. Ironically, he will use the necklace to commemorate her "beauty."

In time, certainly, the boy will become a part of the adult world, but the adult's tendency to differentiate according to superficial factors—race, class, attractiveness—is already evident in the boy's constantly correcting Pacey's grammar and pronunciation. Thus, time—the approach of the adult world—already encroaches upon Pacey and the boy's relationship. Significantly, it is when the boy looks back at the apparently undiminished cowslip field and remarks, "There's just as many as when we came. . . . You'd think we'd never been, wouldn't you?" (15), thus affirming a childish belief in a changeless, timeless world, that Pacey foregoes her condescending, almost cynical air and joyfully swings him round and round. At the end, in his dizziness and innocence, the boy sees an almost mystical aura of beauty about Pacey: "The cowslip field was rolling like a golden sea in the sun and there was a great trembling about Pacey's hair, her necklace and her little crown of gold" (16). It is at once the most beautiful and, because it depends so much on the transience of youth, the most pathetic image in the story.

This same feeling of pathos mingled with haunting beauty underlies most of the *The Watercress Girl* stories. The loneliness, failure of passion, and disorientation in a society in change that dominated the characters in *Colonel Julian* and *The Daffodil Sky* are countered only by the mythic figure of Uncle Silas and the delicate, ephemeral, naive world of *The Watercress Girl*. The respite from harsh reality is brief, as *The Enchantress and Other Stories* demonstrates.

The Enchantress and Other Stories (1961)

The Enchantress and Other Stories (published in England under the title *Now Sleeps the Crimson Petal and Other Stories*) takes up once more Bates's examination of a postwar world of enervating change, crushing loneliness, and wasted passion. Not one of the stories ends happily. Only "Daughters of the Village"—a splendidly written glimpse into an interlude in the lives of a group of rough country women—and "The Enchantress"—the tale of a veritable earth-goddess who is superior to the sorrows, and joys, of the mass of men—escape being totally bleak.

As most reviewers note, Bates lavishly and lovingly paints the atmosphere throughout most of the volume. Occasionally the atmosphere will be as bleak as the theme, as in "Lost Ball." The wasteland landscape is the perfect backdrop for this excellent but painful little tale of a golfer who diligently searches for a lost ball but finds instead a young woman who is apparently contemplating suicide. Unwilling to involve himself in another's life and, in truth, more interested in finding his ball anyway, the golfer abandons the girl when she most needs compassion. As he walks away, the last image demonstrates the blending of setting and theme: "It was exactly as if the sea sometimes held its breath and then broke into a little fragile, broken song."[7]

"Where the Cloud Breaks" is another excellent story that uses atmosphere effectively, but here the atmosphere serves as counterpoint to the theme, thus heightening by contrast. "Where the Cloud Breaks" is particularly interesting since it offers a variation on the theme of the pain caused by cultural change. Colonel Gracie is a retired officer whose distaste for the advances of civilization is so great that he virtually shuts himself off from the world in his country cottage. He forgets the day of the week; he has no modern appliances; he has even canceled his newspaper.

The Colonel's only link with the outside world is through his neighbor, Miss Wilkinson. But even with her he communicates largely by raising flags. Still, the Colonel recognizes, with apprehension, some stirrings of love and desire for her. One day Miss Wilkinson invites him to tea, and tender feelings stir him once more. All this ends, however, when she proudly displays her new acquisition: a television set. Television obviously embodies the worst features of modern technological society for Colonel Gracie, and he becomes obnoxious in his outrage. Miss Wilkinson tells him, in effect, not to bother coming back.

The Colonel returns to his cottage, which is surrounded by his beloved flowers and gardens. Across the way workers are starting to erect Miss Wilkinson's television antenna. It seems that we once more have a clear dichotomy between nature on the one hand and artificiality on the other; but the Colonel has virtually sealed himself away from the world and any chance for love and passion in a cottage of flowers. Obviously, technology itself is not to blame for the evils of modern society; Miss

Wilkinson is after all a normal, healthy woman. It is the inability to adjust to change that is so painful. Miss Wilkinson insists, "There are other viewpoints. One comes to realize that" (126), but the Colonel is single-minded, a doomed relic. The last image of the story makes clear that he does not represent nature. The Colonel stares across the way to Miss Wilkinson's house: "His eyes were blank. They seemed to be groping in immeasurable appeal for something and as if in answer to it the long row of great yellow sunflower faces, the seeds of which were so excellent for the hens, stared back at him, in that wide, laughing, almost mocking way that sunflowers have" (128).

"Now Sleeps the Crimson Petal" is the most ambitious story in the collection. It draws together the major themes that have attracted Bates in the later years: the changing society, numbing loneliness, and the failure of passion.

As is often the case in the later stories, war and its sometimes subtle, always pernicious effects hover in the background. Clara Corbett, the protagonist, carries a memorial to the war with her always in the form of an old rain-cape that wrapped around her face during a bomb blast and saved her, or so she believes, from injury or death.

Clara, bovine and inarticulate, wastes away in a lifeless marriage to a mediocre, mercenary butcher. She encounters a totally new kind of life, however, in the person of rich, foppish Henry Lafarge, to whom she delivers meat at his country estate. She is swept away by his constant chatter, his polished manners, his facile endearments. She obviously thinks him quite democratic, but the reader notices his comments in passing on "lackeys" and "menials."

Clara is totally confused by this strange type of man. When he asks her to bring him one of "her hearts" on her next visit, her embarrassment shows that she believes he has something a bit more romantic in mind than a beef heart. This little incident is emblematic of the confusion between passion and sterility throughout the story. Although Lafarge calls Clara "my heart specialist" (64), he (and the society he represents) has no heart to tend.

Lafarge's caprice climaxes when he swoons in rapture over an artificial rose adorning an old hat of Clara's. He conceives the notion of pinning the rose to some rose bushes which he has planted and shining a light on it as the crowning event of his house-warming. Darling Clara, of course, simply must be there. The thought of attending a party with a crowd of people so obviously above her station agonizes Clara; and we begin to see her as something of a tired old flower, humiliatingly thrust into the spotlight herself. She "felt as if she were under an arc-light,

about to undergo an operation, naked, transfixed, and utterly helpless"
(62–63).

The party is a travesty of bitchy, gossipy women and simpering,
ineffectual men. Clara flounders out of her element; and we sense
something of that brittle, achingly hollow ambience that pervades many
of Katharine Mansfield's stories, as if the flux of experience were moving
just a heartbeat too fast for the protagonist, who tries desperately—not
to make any real sense of it—just to keep from being swept away in the
flood: "She stood in a maze, only half hearing, only half awake. Splin-
ters of conversation went crackling past her bewildered face like scraps of
flying glass" (65).

When Lafarge unveils the artificial rose, Clara finds herself thrust into
the spotlight. Vicious catcalls of "Kiss her! Kiss her!" cascade down, and
Lafarge—despite many hints that women are not the sex that most
interests him—does so, clumsily. As the others trail back into the house,
Clara unties the rose and leaves. Although she still is totally inarticulate,
we sense that she is stunned and humiliated almost beyond grief. But on
the way home, she drops the rose into a ditch and weeps. At the end she
pulls the rain-cape over her head and buries her face in it, "as in a shroud"
(70).

How far has postwar England fallen in Bates's estimation? If "Now
Sleeps the Crimson Petal" is any indication, the fall rivals Adam's. The
landed gentry—which we earlier saw degenerating to a humiliating
state in "The Flag"—has by now been replaced entirely by rich, snobbish, intellectual fops who have no intimate, working relationship with
the land or its people. True passion has withered to its husk, concupiscence, or merely gossip about concupiscence. And Bates's beloved
nature—so warmly invoked in Tennyson's poem "Now Sleeps the Crimson Petal"—has devolved into a plastic rose.

Four Late Collections

The Fabulous Mrs. V (1964), *The Wedding Party* (1965), and *The Wild
Cherry Tree* (1968) are Bates's last collections of short stories before his
death in 1974. A fourth, *The Yellow Meads of Asphodel*, was published
posthumously in 1976. Sparingly reviewed, often not even listed among
Bates's collections in reference works, none could be considered major
efforts. Although each contains some interesting tales, none of the
selections rivals "Now Sleeps the Crimson Petal" or many of the stories
from *Colonel Julian* or *The Daffodil Sky*.

Despite the rather disappointing level of accomplishment in the four works, it is not entirely true that, after four decades and over a dozen collections of short stories, Bates has nothing new to say and no new way to say it. On the contrary, *The Wedding Party* especially offers some interesting developments stylistically and thematically.

For instance, although several of the stories in *The Wedding Party* continue Bates's exploration of loneliness and the failure of passion, more than half are humorous or, more important, optimistic thematically. Indeed, the Uncle Silas volumes aside, *The Wedding Party* is easily the lightest in tone of Bates's career. Two of the stories, to be sure, are new Uncle Silas tales, and two others—"Early One Morning" and "Captain Poop-deck's Paradise"—range from flimsy to farcical. But at least three others are solid, carefully crafted efforts.

"The Sun of December," for example, explores an afternoon in the lives of three septuagenarians, but without the hint of elegy or pathos that many—Bates included—so often reserve for the aged. Indeed, the most entertaining aspect of the story is the debilitation of aging, which Bates presents with humor and understanding. Wolfie, arthritic friend of the narrator, laments, "I am so old . . . that the only way I can get out of a damn taxi is to crawl out backwards, on my hands and knees."[8] And we can do no more than smile at old Mrs. Arkwright as she sips sherry, "spilling some of it down the uppermost of her three powdery chins" (104). In fact, the three characters' physical allowances to age—for instance, Wolfie's standing "erect as he could get himself, balancing between the table and the chair" (104)—only underscore their zest and liveliness. Thus, Mrs. Arkwright's flirtations with the narrator entertain us not through any condescending irony at the senile and infertile old woman, but just the opposite, because we realize that the fires still burn as fiercely as ever.

"The Old Eternal" presents much the same affirmation in the midst of old age as does "The Sun of December," but in a more specifically contemporary context. Here we find pessimistic Mr. Ackerly contrasted to old but vigorous Miss Rigby (Spud) and Miss Pinkerton (Pinky). Mr. Ackerly has dropped into their home—actually a remodeled bomb shelter—for his annual visit, but on Christmas Eve instead of the more customary Christmas Day. He hates to delay anything; with the "bomb" and all, who knows what tomorrow might bring? But the two old ladies' "Happy Christmas to everybody! Let 'em all come! And to ruddy hell with the bomb!" (168) drowns out his nay-saying. At the end Spud and Pinky are left alone; they gaze up at the sky, and Pinky sighs that the stars "look so eternal somehow." Spud agrees: "That's the way they always look to me. . . . But then I like to think we're a bit of the old eternal too" (169).

"The Courtship" is more somber in tone but represents the most fundamental affirmation of the power of love in Bates's canon. The story begins as the narrator encounters an exhausted Bill Browning, who is pushing a cartload of flowers up the street. As the narrator helps him push, Bill tells his story. In brief, Bill had courted Edna for fifteen years, waiting for her mother to die before Edna will marry him. Both lived in indigent circumstances, but Bill gave Edna four shillings a week to treat herself to a good meal. Unfortunately, Edna died before her mother. The cart of flowers, we learn, is Bill's memorial to Edna, who had saved his four shillings a week to give back to him on their wedding day. The irony is predictable, but Bill's reaction is not. Instead of grieving miserably over his loss, he realizes that his life has been enriched and ennobled by love. At the end Bill gives the narrator a white hyacinth, which he carries off before him down the street: "It was exactly like a steadfast fragrant candle, pure and white as snow, lighting the outer darkness" (124).

The title story, "The Wedding Party," shares none of the affirming spirit of the aforementioned. On the contrary, it represents something of a departure for Bates in its strangely disturbing undercurrent of almost Nathanael Westian decadence and incipient violence. The story concerns a young man vacationing in the Alps who encounters a savagely jubilant wedding party and runs off with the bride's sardonic, perhaps psychotic sister, who in the end is forcibly torn from him by brutally gay members of the wedding party.

Neither the plot nor the characterization, however, is as striking as the disturbing ambience in which events occur. Much of this is due to the violent imagery, for instance Bates's description of the approach of the steamer containing the wedding party: "Below the steamer seemed abruptly to be cut in half, partially concealed by some promontory on the shore, and then disappeared altogether" (26). Even more violent, Bates's description of the seizure of the girl strikes us as the savage prelude to some sacrificial rite:

More like a pack of hunting dogs now the squad, suddenly catching sight of her, broke into disordered running, whooping and laughing. She gave him a single desperate kiss and then they were in for the kill, drunk and triumphant, yelling with evil idiocy, seizing her bodily and picking her up. In that moment all his rage came seething back and he started shouting: "God, you bastards! You bastards! You bastards!" flailing about with his fists. A second later, a bottle hit him behind one ear. He dropped to his knees, half-stunned, and when he finally got to his feet again he knew it was no use any longer. They were already at the foot of the slope, running madly, carrying her away shoulder high, like someone on a bier. (44)

We never see the girl again. We never know if her wild accusations against her sister's in-laws are fact or psychotic fancy. We only know that in "The Wedding Party" Bates has constructed a story on the shifting foundation of looming violence and dread.

Neither *The Fabulous Mrs. V* nor *The Wild Cherry Tree*, nor the posthumously published *The Yellow Meads of Asphodel*, offers anything new thematically or stylistically. The pessimistic themes—loneliness, inhibited passion, sordid and joyless sex—that prevailed throughout much of the later years of his career underlie most of the stories. An author does not automatically fail simply by exploring again and again aspects of a theme or related themes. Many great authors—James, Lawrence, and Hemingway come immediately to mind—spend major phases or entire careers in variations on a common theme. But when an author fails to find any refreshing method to approach his theme or fresh story to embody it, the reader grows restive. Whether because he used his themes to exhaustion or for some other reason, Bates's powers as a storyteller fail him in many of the selections in *The Fabulous Mrs. V*, *The Wild Cherry Tree*, and *The Yellow Meads of Asphodel*.

The relatively disappointing level of accomplishment in Bates's last four collections of short stories should not obscure the fact that by as late as 1961 *(The Enchantress and Other Stories)* Bates was writing some of his most effective short stories. This is after three and one-half decades of writing and publishing short fiction . The continuing strength of Bates's short fiction, particularly in contrast to his later novels, lends further support to the conclusion that the short story was not only Bates's first love, but also his most enduring and fruitful one.

Chapter Seven
The Novel in the Later Years (1951—74)

If Bates's short stories in the later years represent a second flowering, it is not because he broke new ground stylistically or grew noticeably in other ways as an artist; rather, he returned to the tried-and-true methods and materials employed in the earlier years of his career. While we applaud the quality and polish of his work, then, we are also aware that he had reached the limits of his capabilities as a writer of short stories.

Much the same can be said for Bates the novelist in the later years, with the reservation that he far less often reached the level of earlier years, as he frequently did in the short story. We may therefore place Bates in a group of novelists—along with Huxley, Waugh, Cary, Compton-Burnett, and so forth—who emerged from World War II with established reputations but who largely failed to test further the possibilities of fiction. British fiction in general stagnated in the years following World War II. Only Graham Greene and William Golding are consistently bestowed the label of "major" figures. (Whether Samuel Beckett is a French or Irish writer is too complex to argue here.)

Only one movement in England gained a measure of notoriety during this period; and perhaps no movement of writers, most of whom deny any part in a definable "school," has been so scorned in English literary history as the "Angry Young Men." Bates had little use for the Angry Young Men; John Osborne's *Look Back in Anger* should have been called *Look Back in Self-Pity*, he scoffed.[1] And generally the scorn is justified. Too often we sense in the Angry Young Men's works that the motivating emotion is not so much anger as mere peevishness or irritation. Worse, we sense that the irritation is directed not at fundamental flaws in English society but at the fact that the protagonists are on the outside of society and want very much to be "in."

Few novelists confronted the spiritual and material problems of postwar England as unflinchingly and harrowingly as did Bates in *Dear Life*, and Bates himself never did again. Of the eleven novels that Bates published between 1952 to 1970, only in the Larkin family series are postwar problems and issues felt to any significant degree. As do the short stories, the best of Bates's novels in the later years take us back to an earlier period, a period with its own tragedy, death, and despair, yet always glowing with the wistful aura of the past.

Love for Lydia (1952)

A good example is *Love for Lydia*, probably the best of Bates's novels in the later years. A few reviewers of *Love for Lydia* complain that the characters are largely static and essentially shallow, that we do not gain enough insight into them to warrant the nearly 350 pages of the novel. There is a degree of truth in the complaint, although at least one of the major characters does grow and mature. Profundity of characterization was never Bates's strength; skillful evocation of time, place, and atmosphere is, and rarely does Bates manage it better than in *Love for Lydia*.

The evocation of setting and mood is so strong because Bates was so intimately involved with his subject. The setting is Evensford, Bates's fictional version of his native Rushden. The time is 1929 and the early years of the 1930s: the years of the protagonist's, and Bates's, young manhood. The protagonist is a young reporter who hates his job and the "stuffy little prison"[2] that is Evensford, a condition that exactly matches Bates's unhappiness as a reporter for the *Northampton Chronicle*. Nearly all of Bates's novels and many of his short stories were inspired by a germ of fact, but *Love for Lydia* is the only one that Bates unabashedly called autobiographical,[3] testament to the author's emotional investment in his material.

Love for Lydia is a novel of the joy, passion, and the pain of young love, but more than that it is a novel of a young man's struggle to understand and resolve himself to a formidable world of change and uncertainty. It has much in common with Bates's novels of the 1930s, novels that explored the effects of time and change on individuals and communities. There are six major characters in the novel: the reporter, who is narrator and protagonist; Lydia, a lovely, cruelly self-centered young woman obsessed with the enjoyment of life at all costs; Alex, a wealthy, cynical young man too much given to drink; Tom, a good-natured young farmer; Nancy, Tom's cow-eyed sister; and Blackie, an inarticulate, brooding young mechanic drawn unwillingly into Lydia's circle. The novel is composed primarily of scenes of dances and parties where first one and then another of the young men fall in love with Lydia, who accepts it all as her due, returns it all with affection and physical love, to the satisfaction of none. Before the novel ends, Alex and Tom

are dead—victims of untempered passion, although not always their
own, and not always involving Lydia directly—and all have been injured
by love misguided or unrequited.

The characters may sound a little "pat" and the situations a trifle
melodramatic, with reason. Yet the characters are, after all, young, as
given to extremes of emotion and action as Juliet and her Romeo. We
recognize them as foolish, yet realistically so, held in thrall by Lydia and
her *carpe diem* philosophy: "If we want to do it we just do it, don't we? I
think it's awfully silly to weigh up things. Let's just do them when we
want to" (45).

The reporter-narrator is the first of the young men to recognize the
destructive self-centeredness of Lydia, the "instinct and feeling and
blood" (131) rather than rationality that drives her. After Alex's and
Tom's deaths he flees to London; when he returns two years later, he
finds that the "slump" had crippled Evensford and Lydia is in a sanitari-
um, victim of a year-long orgy. Her primary problem, a doctor tells the
reporter, is loneliness. He recognizes that an unconquerable loneliness is
what has driven her all along, but he realizes even more about himself: "I
had so often thought of her growing up from something awkward and
lonely, that it had not occurred to me that I had been growing up, just as
painfully, in the same way. It had not occurred to me that the pain of
love might be a part of its flowering" (343). What his hatred of his job
and community, his fear of Lydia and love, his pointless flight to London
amount to is simply a fear of life itself. With that realization comes the
thought that he, in his jealousy and moodiness and absence during her
most painful year, might have caused Lydia as much pain as she caused
him. The novel ends in his committing himself to Lydia in a far more
mature and lasting fashion than he was capable of at the story's beginning.

The narrator undergoes a process of maturing and change, then, even
if we are not so sure that Lydia has. But the narrator's is not the only
transformation in the novel. Equally interesting is the more subtle
changes in Evensford and rural England. These are the changes that have
the deepest impact on the "older" narrator, and actually the novel does
have two narrators. One is the young reporter: self-centered, naive,
unaware. The other is an older, wiser man looking back at the naive self
decades distant, recognizing changes that the younger man not only
could not have seen but would not, in his young cynicism, have cared
about. Phrases such as "in those days" signal us that the focus is
broadening to include an historical perspective, as when the narrator
recalls a line of elms leading to Lydia's house "killed as sure as poison
twenty-three years later" (53) by concrete tank implacements.

Virtually any reasonably competent writer of popular novels could have given us the story of Lydia and her young men. Only Bates, though, through his older narrator, could give us such an evocative picture of what it was like to be young and in love in the English Midlands in the years of the Jazz Age and the "slump." "I had a text on my bedroom wall which told me that God was the unseen listener to every conversation," recalls the narrator, "but the walls were so thin that we could hear the conversations of the Pendletons [neighbors] too and the sizzle of kippers in their frying pans" (10). The narrator recalls the past not always with wistfulness; most often we are given an accurate and unsentimentalized view of how time transformed Evensford (Rushden) from a country village of eight hundred souls in 1820 to a grimy factory town of thousands a century later: "Long rows of bright red brick, of houses roofed with slate shining like blue steel, had rapidly eaten their way beyond the shabby confines of what had been a village, beyond new railway tracks and gasworks, obliterating pleasant outlying farms and hedgerows of hawthorn and wild rose" (12).

It is the incidental descriptions and observations—the girl who is beaten by her Presbyterian father for cutting her hair in the latest style; the hauntingly nostalgic walk that the narrator takes at night with an old school chum shortly before both are to leave Evensford; the sights, sounds, and smells of everyday existence in a factory town—that elevate *Love for Lydia* above the merely popular novel that a brief summary of its plot and characters would seem to indicate. This feel for the sensory texture of time and place is what always characterizes Bates's work at its best. *Love for Lydia* showed that, at least once in his later novels, Bates could rekindle the old creative fires.

The Feast of July (1954)

Happily, *Love for Lydia* was not the last of Bates's exemplary novels. His next, *The Feast of July*, also draws on the materials and methods that characterized his work in the early years of his career. In fact, had we not known its copyright date, its nostalgic tone, beautiful descriptions of nature, late-nineteenth-century setting, and simplicity of design and language would probably cause us to conclude that the novel is contemporary with *The Two Sisters*, Bates's first.

The novel's opening sentence indicates that Bates's methods and prose will be simple and direct: "She was looking for a man named Arch Wilson and she was walking northwestward, alone, towards the middle of the country, with another fifty or sixty miles to go."[4] The "she" is Bella Ford, a simple country girl who was seduced, impregnated, then abandoned by smooth-talking Arch Wilson. All her cross-country march to the shoemaking town of Nenweald (where Arch reportedly lives) brings her is a miscarriage and near starvation. But at Nenweald she is taken in by the Wainwright family. Over the course of the next year each of the three Wainwright brothers falls in love with her, but after one leaves for the army and another runs off to London, she is left to brooding, inarticulate, but sensitive Con, who loved her first and most fiercely all along. Their potential happiness is upset by the reappearance of Arch on Feast Sunday, the first Sunday in July when the farmers celebrate the first green peas and new potatoes of the year. In a rage, Con kills Arch, and then he and Bella flee across the countryside. Driven nearly insane by guilt, Con gives himself up to the police and is sentenced to ten years in prison; the novel ends with Bella returning to her home, prepared to wait for Con's release.

The Feast of July is not the first Bates work that seems strongly indebted to an author whom Bates largely detested: Thomas Hardy. The naive girl made pregnant by the slick villain, the rural setting and seasonal rhythms, the inevitable violence, the flight with the lover and his eventual capture—all are variations on Tess of the d'Urbervilles. If Bates's novel does not have the power, scope, and complexity of Tess, it is interesting in its own way. Bella is a victim of circumstance, to be sure, but she is not merely a whimpering plaything of fate. Proud, strong, resilient, Bella "gave the impression of being taller than she was, walking with her head back" (16). She survives a betrayal and miscarriage, the indifference of her own mother, the jealousy of a potential mother-in-law, the death of her closest friend (Nell, Con's sister), the murder of her former lover, and the imprisonment of the man who was to be her husband. And her survival is not numb and bovine, but conscious and resolute. At the end of the novel we leave Bella on a train returning to her home, knowing that she cannot see her lover for ten years, yet confident and serene.

As was the case with Love for Lydia, the strengths of The Feast of July are not in its plot, characterization, or theme. The plot is rather predictable, after all, and the characters are all people we have seen before. It is the richly textured cultural and historical milieu within which the characters act and interact, together with Bates's accustomed polished prose, that makes The Feast of July memorable. Like the Evensford of so many of Bates's works, which itself is patterned after his native Rushden, Nenweald is a shoemaking town, the product of the industrial revolution but still conscious of its rural heritage. The Wainwrights, for instance, are all shoemakers, and they live in one of the hundreds of featureless row houses: "Number Sixteen of thirty in a row. Beyond the asphalt yards were strips of garden, dark after winter, and then the brick two-storey shops beyond" (31). Bella, from near the coast, cannot shut out the noise of the "hammering of shoemakers working from daybreak and on into the night, by the light of little tin oil lamps, in the dark-windowed shops all along the row" (31).

What Bates so accurately describes is not simply Bella's adopted home, but the Rushden of his and his father's youth. It is the influence of this recollected reality, even more than the fact that the story is technically told in retrospect, that gives the novel its elegiac tone. The novel is not blatantly nostalgic, however, and neither is it oblivious to the harsh realities of that vanished world. The shoemaking industry itself was a dreary business, at the whim of the seasons and an uncertain economy. The winters in particular were cruel times, with little or no work to be had. It was on the bleakest of these winter days that young Nell Wainwright ran for ten miles pulling an iron truck, following a rumor of shoes to be made. When she gets there, she finds that a neighbor arrived just moments before and has been given all the leather "uppers" for shoes. She then runs another ten miles pursuing another rumor, waits for hours in the numbing cold, and is rewarded with a grand total of six "uppers." Nell contracts rheumatic fever shortly afterward and dies. We do not know if the incident has any basis in fact, but it has the feel of a grim actuality with which the author was all too familiar.

In his autobiography, Bates recalls when he was writing and publishing his novels of the Far East how fervently some of his friends wished him to return to the familiar Midlands for his materials. In the early 1950s Bates seems consciously to be granting that wish, with two fine novels of Midland life. But when he embarked upon a third, *The Sleepless Moon*, the once-fertile ground seems to have been worked to sterility.

The Sleepless Moon (1956)

If *Dear Life* ranks as Bates's most undervalued, neglected novel, *The Sleepless Moon* occupies the opposite end of the pole. Several reviewers praise it highly; one, astoundingly, calls it Bates's best novel. A smaller number of reviewers find it interminable, repetitive, lifeless, and dull. In this case, unfortunately, the minority rules.

To any close follower of Bates's works, the plot of *The Sleepless Moon* will sound all too familiar. A painfully shy young woman, Constance, marries an equally shy older man, Melford, who is far more interested in his grocery business than he is in her. He never manages, in fact, to consummate the marriage. Constance endures several months of this passionless existence, and the reader too many chapters, until she meets Frankie, a shallow young man with a mocking smile, who promptly seduces her. Their sex affair (it cannot be called love affair) lasts for several hundred pages, until Frankie's passion cools and his brother-in-law throws him out of the house. He leaves town but then returns later with the thought of starting up his old affairs (he has had several). But by this time Constance has discovered that she is not the only star in Frankie's skies. Finally realizing how empty and miserable her past has been and how bleak her prospects are, Constance leaps out of her local church tower to her death.

The idea of the unhappy young woman stuck in a passionless marriage to an insensitive husband and failing to find happiness with an oily young wastrel is one that Bates used in far too many works. In fact, *The Sleepless Moon* is little more than a tiresome and insipid reworking of *Catherine Foster*. Bates himself sketched the parallels between the two novels in his autobiography (*World in Ripeness,* 122—24), blithely unaware that the similarities were so close as to make the later novel redundant.

There are a few interesting scenes and passages in the novel, almost none of which directly involves our protagonist, Constance. But that is the problem. Bates has chosen to construct one of his longest novels around a character who is too shallow and hopeless to maintain our interest for more than a few chapters. Her lover is such a predictable caricature that we never for a moment see him as a possible answer to her problems, so we lose hope far sooner than Constance does. The only character of any depth or complexity is Melford, and Melford obviously lacks his creator's sympathies (and thus ours as well).

The Sleepless Moon is another indication of Bates's writing too much, too quickly. In four years he had written three novels and a number of short stories and novellas, all set in the Midlands. This was too much, even for a writer of Bates's vast energy. *The Sleepless Moon* seems more the product of exhaustion than inspiration.

The Novels of the Larkin Family

Bates never read the many good reviews of *The Sleepless Moon*. A close and respected friend was so dismayed by the novel's sexual license (certainly mild by today's standards) that, in a fit of artistic depression, Bates vowed to give up the novel. It was not his first such vow, and this one lasted all of two years. When he returned to the novel in 1958, it was to begin a series of five novels recording the Chaucerian (Bates's term) exploits and Rabelaisian appetites of a junk-dealing family from Kent: the Larkins. The first of what was to become Bates's most popular works was *The Darling Buds of May* (1958), followed by *A Breath of French Air* (1959), *Hark, Hark, the Lark* (1960; originally published in England as *When the Green Woods Laugh*), *Oh! to Be in England* (1963), and finally *A Little of What You Fancy* (1970), Bates's last novel.

Pop, the patriarch of the Larkin family, is a cold-war reincarnation of the irrepressible Uncle Silas. Both flout conventional wisdom and morality in hot pursuit of the good life, and both prosper in their own ways. If Uncle Silas was patterned after Bates's uncle Joe Betts, Pop resembles no one so closely as Bates's image of himself: " . . . there is something of myself in Pop Larkin: a passionate Englishman, a lover of nature, of the sounds and sights of the countryside, of colour, flowers and things sensual; a hatred of pomp, pretension and humbug; a lover of children and family life; an occasional breaker of rules, a flouter of conventions. . . . Pop is in fact an expression of my own philosophy: the need to go with the stream, never to battle against it" (*World in Ripeness*, 152).

Pop Larkin represents Bates's clearest fictional embodiment of his philosophy, a philosophy that makes a religion of the total enjoyment of all appetites. In *A Breath of French Air*, Pop muses that if he had to define his religion,". . . he would say that being alive was his relidge [*sic*]— that and earth and woods and flowers and nightingales and all that sort of lark and enjoying it and not preventing other people from doing so."[5] This seems an innocent philosophy, not likely to offend; but in the cold-war years of the 1950s, when conformity was the rule and law, Pop Larkin offends a great many. And despite Bates's disclaimer, Pop was hardly one to simply "go with the stream" of public opinion. In a certain respect the Larkin novels are Bates's answer to the "Angry Young Men" fiction of Amis, Wain, and the rest; instead of sniveling about the state of sorry old England, the Larkins carve out their niche of Eden, albeit in a junk pile. Thus, when in *A Little of What You Fancy* Sir Furlington-Snow, Queen's Counsel, contemplates the glorious excess of the Larkin's lifestyle, "It seemed to him to be, among other things, part of the answer to a mad world."[6]

The Larkin novels in general have only a hint of structure or plot and very little conflict. What conflict there is is always between the Larkin philosophy of the good life and someone else who thoughtlessly espouses a more traditional and inhibited one. The conflict climaxes when the

representative of conventional society is won over or shocked into
retreat. In true comic fashion, each novel ends with a marriage or the
announcement of an impending one, or at the very least the establish-
ment of a sexual liaison, plus in most cases Ma Larkin's happy realization
that she is pregnant again, and in each case a grand feast where all
partake of Gargantuan quantities of food, drink, and sex.

  The Darling Buds of May sets the pattern for the Larkin novels. It opens
with Ma's pronouncement that their oldest daughter, Mariette, is
pregnant, father unknown. Pop's response indicates his philosophy:
"Oh? . . . Well, that don't matter. Perfick [*sic*]. Jolly good."[7] The
conflict soon enters in the person of Mr. Charlton, a tax collector. It
seems Pop has never paid taxes, having been too busy raising pigs to fool
with the forms. Mr. Charlton is not only a representative of the govern-
ment, but also of that vast majority who devote so much energy to their
jobs that they have none at all left over for "living." It does not take Mr.
Charlton long to be first shocked, then dazed, and finally won over by
the generous plenitude of the Larkins. Stuffed with food, nearly drowned
in alcohol, seduced by Mariette, Mr. Charlton never goes back to his job.
Not only are the tax forms forgotten, but Mariette's "problem" is taken
care of when she and Charlton announce their engagement at the end.
This announcement causes Ma and Pop vaguely to wonder if it is not
time for them to get married also, especially now that Ma is again
pregnant, with their seventh child. But Mr. Charlton advises against
it: marriage would only increase their taxes.

  There are many additional characters and side-plots in *The Darling
Buds of May*, the majority having very little to do with the Charlton—
Mariette—income-tax conflict, and that is the pattern for all the Larkin
novels. Whatever seems to be the central conflict occupies the stage for
only a small part of the time: often less than half. The remainder is
devoted to glimpses of Pop's ongoing flirtations with a variety of women
old and young (Ma approves, not averse to a little "variety" herself), his
almost honest, always lucrative dealings in the junk trade, and the
family's insatiable appetite for food and drink, feast and seduction.

  The only thing resembling a conflict in *A Breath of French Air* is the
dreary weather and awful food at a French seaside resort where the
Larkins, plus Charlton, go to escape a chilly English summer. Needless
to say, the Larkins simply will not have any dreariness on their vacation,
and the weather is soon bright and sunny and the food, drink, and
flirtation abundant. When they leave at the end of their visit—without
eleven-year-old Primrose, who is going to stay for a time with her twelve-
year-old boyfriend—they have not so much Anglicized as Larkinized a

bit of France. And France, even more than England, needs help. A certain repulsive rather than amusing flavor of Francophobia pervades the novel. The natives are always "Froggies" rather than French. (In a later Larkin novel, *Oh! to Be in England*, Pop shrugs, "After all, Froggies are human, I suppose, Ma. In a way."[8])

The third Larkin novel, *Hark, Hark, the Lark*, is more interesting than *A Breath of French Air* because it has a more clearly defined conflict. The conflict, as always, concerns the Larkins versus convention, this time in the person of Mr. and Mrs. Jerebohm. The Jerebohms are rich and snobbish Londoners who have purchased a baronial estate that Pop had earlier acquired from the original inhabitants who, like so many in contemporary England, could no longer afford the taxes and maintenance. The Jerebohms' avowed intention in buying the estate, other than acquiring a status symbol, is to lose money: a tax "lark." Ma feels that there is something not quite right about this practice, apparently forgetting Pop's far more questionable relationship to the tax authorities. Bates gives us a great deal of good humor around the well-worked theme of the city folk being duped by the country folk—the Larkins are, after all, an English version of Ma and Pa Kettle—and the novel climaxes when Pop is taken to court by Mrs. Jerebohm for "violating" her: a charge of which Pop is guilty in intent if not in fact.

It all turns out well, as we knew it would all along, thanks to a little manipulation on Bates's part. But then we do not expect aesthetic masterpieces in the Larkin novels: just good, if not so "clean," fun. It all goes to prove, as a friend of Pop's says, "If you're going to be raped . . . you might as well relax and enjoy it while you can."[9] And that goes to prove that we do not expect to find moral or philosophical profundity in the Larkin novels, either.

Oh! to Be in England brings Mademoiselle Dupont over from France—where she owned the resort visited by the Larkins in *A Breath of French Air*—for the christening of John Marlborough Churchill Blenheim, Charlton and Mariette's new baby. The only problem is that no christening is planned. In fact, none of the Larkins has ever been christened, Pop's religion being "natural" rather than institutional. Pop and Ma decide that the whole clan might as well be done at once, and this brings Reverend Candy, one of our two "conformist" characters, on the scene. The other is the bullying, snobbish Captain Broadbent; and after a great deal of drinking, feasting, and flirting, the former is recruited as a Larkin disciple while the latter retreats in shock.

One other conflict adds a darker hue to this by now quite predictable Larkin canvas: the occasional appearance of vicious, violent young men and women. These are the "Teddy boys" of postwar England, the disaffected youth who rebelled against English society by flouting its laws and customs. The Larkins do much the same thing, of course, but their means are harmless and their ends are simple pleasure. The Teddy boys are finally routed physically from the scene by Reverend Candy, drawing upon his experience in London's East End. A hammerlock is no solution to a complex social and economic problem, certainly, but the Teddy boys are but a small black cloud in the blue skies of the Larkin world. The novel ends in typical fashion, with Ma's announcement that she's pregnant yet again.

Published in 1970, *A Little of What You Fancy* is both the final Larkin novel and the last novel in Bates's career. Here, appropriately, the conflict is the final one for us all: death itself. The novel opens with Ma and Pop in bed just after dawn, sipping champagne and preparing to make love for the third time. But the third time is curtailed when Pop suffers a heart attack. Worse than the attack itself is the doctor's prescription for recovery: no excitement (sex), strict diet, and no alcohol, perhaps forever. Pop lapses into glum depression, but Ma is outraged at this unnatural regimen. Her outrage finds a target in Nurse Soper, grim and dictatorial, who Pop claims should have been a nun: "Never want none, never give none and never had none" (80). Nurse Soper is soon replaced by the beautiful and more understanding Nurse Trevelyan, but Pop only sinks deeper into his swamp of self-pity.

Anger is what Pop needs to give him life, all decide, as a plot is hatched to involve Pop emotionally in the salvation of merry old England. It seems that plans are afoot to build a tunnel across the Channel from France to England, destroying England's hallowed status as an island. It is the work of the devil, old Miss Barnwell avows: "Whether you call him Common Market, Rome, decimal, Channel Tunnel, Europe, Centigrade, or whatever" (151). A threat to his beloved England is bad enough, but when Pop learns that an access highway to the tunnel would run right across his junkyard, all self-pity is forgotten. After a great deal of bullying, bribery, and chicanery, plans for the tunnel are delayed for several decades, probably forever. The novel ends with Ma inviting Pop into her bed, doctor's orders or no, having determined never to sleep by herself again, and promising to give Pop "A little of what you fancy" (162).

No works of Bates's career so polarized reviewers as the Larkin novels. Half found them hilarious, unpretentious, and delightful. Most of the remainder found them shrill, artificial, repetitious, and juvenile. All the adjectives, good and bad, apply at various times. At the very least, to be enjoyed the Larkin novels must be approached in the proper spirit. We cannot expect profundity of characterization or theme, sophistication of plot or structure. By the time Bates began the Larkin series his best novels were behind him. We can expect to find an author trying mightily to entertain us. He succeeds often and fails often, the exact proportion depending upon our ability, like Pop and his creator, "to go with the stream, never to battle against it."

A Crown of Wild Myrtle (1962), *A Moment in Time* (1964), and *The Distant Horns of Summer* (1967)

Three novels of widely varying subjects and settings interspersed the years of the Larkin novels. All are more somber than the Larkin novels, providing their author with needed relief, perhaps, from the desperate good humor of the junk dealer.

The first of these is *A Crown of Wild Myrtle* (1962). Although a story of suspense, violence, and lesbianism set in the Greek isles during the Cuban missile crisis of 1962, *A Crown of Wild Myrtle* shares at least one thing with the Larkin series. All are what is now sometimes termed in the publishing world "summer" fiction: works meant to be "a good read," in which the reader is quickly and easily engaged, and then the work just as quickly forgotten. One expects a certain slickness of plot and facileness of characterization with no intruding hint of profundity of any sort, and *A Crown of Wild Myrtle* qualifies just as well as the Larkin novels.

One of the primary qualities of "summer" fiction is that our lines of sympathy must be clearly drawn. In this case, Englishman Jack Marsden quite clearly wears the white hat. The middle-aged, shrewish, possessive, lesbian, and finally psychotic Mrs. Keller is—from the first moment that we hear her shrill, berating voice to the last when she commits suicide, having failed to murder Jack—the villain. In between is Mrs. Keller's young and lovely "traveling companion," poor Ruth Forbes, whom Jack must save from the older woman's clutches. *A Crown of Wild Myrtle* is but an exotic variation of Bates's well-worn pattern of the inhibited young woman being introduced to passion and love by a more experienced man.

With *A Crown of Wild Myrtle* Bates unabashedly moves back into the realm of the popular novel. It is a fast-paced novel—curiously, there is really very little action—and the at once beautiful and decaying villages of the Greek isles add to the air of romance and suspense that Bates, skillful as ever, weaves so masterfully. But the novel does have its flaws, even for popular fiction. Perhaps bold in 1962, the lesbian affair would probably strike today's reader as too much of a literary cliché. And Bates throughout his career never could convincingly capture American dialogue (Ruth and Mrs. Keller are Americans). Few working-class girls from Baltimore have ever used the phrase, "I daresay," and probably none in history has described her affection for a young man with the words, "I was the great one for him too. . . . "[10] The setting does come to life for us, although the many allusions to and inferences of Greek myth are more decorative than fundamental to theme, tone, or characterization. Jack, Ruth, and Mrs. Keller have more the flat sketchiness of fairy-tale figures than the stature of myth.

But these are minor complaints about a novel whose aim was not very lofty, after all. *A Crown of Wild Myrtle* was meant to be a pleasant pastime for a summer's day, and this it does admirably.

Bates probably visualized *A Moment in Time* (1964) as a weightier, more important work than *A Crown of Wild Myrtle*, and in some ways it is. Bates's object is not merely to tell us an interesting tale to help us while away an afternoon but to recapture an historic moment in time: the summer and fall of 1940 when England endured the Battle of Britain, and finally triumphed. Because the aim of the novel is greater, however, its flaws are also magnified; and we leave *A Moment in Time* less satisfied on the whole than we were with *A Crown of Wild Myrtle*.

The novel is told in retrospect, through the point of view of Elizabeth, a young woman in the South of England to whom, at the beginning of the novel, the "war seemed unreal anyway. I was a girl and I wasn't part of it."[11] To her family—her fatuous mother, even more fatuous Uncle Henry, and strong and witty Grandmother—the war is even more distant. "The notion of making one's toast by the fire was, for our family at any rate, still an unthinkable one" (9). The war, or at least the military, becomes more of a reality when officers come to requisition the family house for an R.A.F. mess. Up unto this point the novel is convincing; we are interested in the characters and share the family's outrage at being forced to vacate their house on forty-eight hours' notice. But problems soon develop.

Not only is Elizabeth telling the story in retrospect, but so is Bates, of course, writing *A Moment in Time* over two decades after he began his duties as Flying Officer 'X.' Despite his intimate knowledge of the grim reality of those early days of the war, the danger is that distance in time will too much temper reality with nostalgia and sentimentality; and Bates succumbs too often. In fairness, he tries mightily to avoid sentimentality. The novel opens with a Dantesque image of swans swimming in a circle of water on an otherwise frozen lake—" . . . a big black hole, a bottomless grave in the glistening sepulchral whiteness of snow" (8)—lending a sense of foreboding to the opening pages of the novel. Terrible things happen to characters of whom Bates has made us fond. In a chilling scene, Elizabeth comes upon what she believes is a dead pilot, hideously mangled, sitting beneath a tree in a meadow; but the "dead" pilot moves, speaks, and she recognizes the voice of an old beau, who is in fact recovering from recent wounds. That scene is paralleled by a later one in which Elizabeth runs after a German pilot whose parachute is drifting down into the nearby woods. When she sees the pilot dangling from a tree—bloody, burned, his intestines hanging out—she realizes that he represents a very unsentimental view of all dead pilots everywhere. Sometime later, her husband of a few short months, himself an R.A.F. pilot, is killed by a random bomb.

Despite his frequent zeal for realism, we cannot help but feel that Bates's ultimate goal is glorification, not faithful depiction. The courage is always a bit too muted and understated, the occasional grief and despair a bit too colorful. The slang—the "prangs" and "gongs" and "wizards"—no doubt is accurate, if nearly incomprehensible to today's readers, but it so gluts the pages of Bates's novel that it makes the characters sound irritatingly adolescent. The sentimentality is the strongest in the final pages of the novel, where Elizabeth most obviously is viewing the action in retrospect, and this is the weakest part of the novel. If the last words are truly those of a woman recalling the days when her young husband was blasted out of the world, then that woman has the soul of a Caesar, not a Cleopatra: " . . . and I know too that there will never be a battle like it again . . . never again" (248). The words are obviously Bates's, not Elizabeth's, words of zeal and nostalgia, not for a dead lover, but for an age of valor and victory.

That bifurcated vision at the end indicates the novel's major flaw. The Battle of Britain itself is the major character, vitiating the struggles, loves, and griefs of the individual men and women in the novel; but since the story is told through the point of view of Elizabeth, we never get a very clear picture of the actuality or scope of the battle either. Neither the microcosm nor the macrocosm comes alive for us; all we are left with is the fuzziness of nostalgia.

Although flawed, the best novel of the three is the last, *The Distant Horns of Summer* (1967). Compared to *A Moment in Time*, the cast of characters is small and the scope and aim of the novel are relatively unambitious. The setting is an English country estate some time after

World War II. The basic pattern of the novel is by this time disturbingly familiar: a young woman has led a passionless life; she has an affair with a more experienced man of nebulous background; he deserts her; she commits suicide. Yet Bates varies the pattern enough to engage us in the characters' fates.

In *The Distant Horns of Summer* either of two characters could be considered our protagonist. At the beginning of the novel our attention centers upon James Sampson, the six-year-old son of parents who evidently consider him more of a bother than an object or source of affection. They spend most of their time searching for the sun in Tangier or wherever, delegating their parental duty by hiring a succession of governesses to care for him in the little cottage in the shadow of the mansion they call home during their short, infrequent visits. James's companionship comes not primarily from the governesses but from Mr. Pimm and Mr. Monday, two friendly, colorful characters whom James has constructed out of his observations, imagination, and need. By the time we encounter James at the beginning of the novel, Mr. Pimm and Mr. Monday are far more real to James than anyone, certainly more real than his parents.

James's situation is not startlingly uncommon in "real" life or original in literature. What is more interesting is the situation of his new governess, Gilly, a young lady hired by James's father expressly because she is not very pretty and therefore unlikely to attract distracting suitors. We soon find that James and Gilly have much in common, psychologically. James sees faces and shapes in the clouds, and Gilly had begun to see faces in the buns that she sold in a bakery. She had given up the bakery job because of a painful infatuation with a customer who was hardly aware of her existence. Thus both James and Gilly are terribly lonely, and soon Gilly joins James in the imaginary world of Mr. Pimm (Mr. Monday spends most of the novel recuperating from a broken arm), automatically setting a place for him at table, taking his part in conversations. By the time Alex Ainsworth appears on the scene, "the emotions now engendered in her as Mr. Pimm's emotions were somehow greater than those she felt as herself."[12] Even after she falls in love with Alex and begins their affair, she cannot totally get Mr. Pimm out of her mind, and she bristles at Alex's jokes about Mr. Pimm.

When the focus shifts to the affair of Gilly and Alex, *The Distant Horns of Summer* becomes too much like a half-dozen other Bates novels; from the first mention of Alex's "mocking" manner—and all of Bates's base males have a mocking manner—we know that the affair is doomed. From the beginning of the affair onward, the novel is interesting and original only insofar as the affair affects the relationship between our two protagonists and only as it precipitates their twin descent into psychosis. At the end Gilly kills herself when she believes that she has been responsible for James's drowning (he was alive and well, hiking toward the sea with Mr. Pimm), but James is reserved for a grimmer fate: continuation in the same lonely, loveless life as the son of absentee parents. The last scene shows James standing beside a new governess, who points to his parents at last coming up the drive toward him. "Who is it?" he asks. "Who are they?" (277).

Temperamental, self-centered, undisciplined—James is not a likable boy, yet Bates causes us to care about him and feel pain at his fate. We did not care about the characters at all in *A Crown of Wild Myrtle*, although we were entertained by the novel; we cared about the characters but felt almost trapped into doing so in *A Moment of Time*; but in *The Distant Horns of Summer* Bates creates a believable world of dreams and illusion, without exotic settings or the hazy focus of sentimentality.

The Distant Horns of Summer is a good work upon which to conclude our discussion of the novel in Bates's later years. Like *The Distant Horns of Summer*, the novels in general in the later years mark no advance in method or content for Bates. In fact, they were best when they drew upon familiar themes, settings, and characters, although this occasionally led Bates to repeating himself to the detriment of a particular work. If we may extend the metaphor that we have used several times to describe Bates's career, if the later years represent a second flowering for Bates the short-story writer, they mark a period of gleaning well-worked fields for Bates the novelist.

Chapter Eight

The Novella
in the Later Years
(1951–74)

Bates had written fictions which might qualify as novellas before the later years of his career, most notably *The Cruise of the Breadwinner* (1946). Yet the sheer number of novellas which he produced between 1953 and 1970—twenty-two, five collections and one published separately—indicates that the novella acquired a fascination for Bates rivaling the novel and the short story. By all accounts the novella is a difficult form in which to work but one whose rewards are great. Bates's praise of the form reflects a recognition of both its challenges and virtues: "Balance without stiffness, economy without cramp, essentials that are not merely bare bones, a canvas of character and scene which, though only a quarter or a tenth of the size of the novel, must nevertheless satisfy the reader just as much and do so perhaps more by what it leaves out than by what it puts in—these are merely a few of the technical challenges that make the *novella* so fascinating to the truly creative artist."[1]

"Novella" is one of the most illusive of literary terms. No definition accounts for all works which we normally consider to be novellas while at the same time excluding all other works of fiction. Generally, the novella accepts the restrictions of the short story—a limited number of characters and a single plot line uncomplicated by detours and sub-plots—while at the same time it partakes of the novel's depth of analysis. It seems an ideal form for a writer of Bates's talents, allowing him to develop characters and situations at somewhat greater length than allowed by the short story yet enabling him for the most part to avoid the flaws that frequently plagued him in the novel: static characters, weak plots, and repetition. Although not each of his novellas is a masterpiece, he succeeded often enough to make himself one of the most prolific and proficient writers of the novella in English since Conrad.

The Nature of Love: Three Short Novels (1953)

Bates's first collection of novellas in the later years was not entirely successful, at least if we can trust a significant number of reviewers. Actually the reviews are a strikingly mixed lot, with one reviewer attacking the very story or technique that the next applauds. Part of the reason for reviewer disenchantment might be the unrelenting pathos of the stories in *The Nature of Love*. We are afforded hardly a glimpse of a peak among the dismal valleys. Indeed, *The Nature of Love* is a curious title for the collection, unless we infer that Bates does in fact have a bleak conception of love. A *Times Literary Supplement* reviewer objects that it is a bit of a coincidence that in each story *both* partners fall in love at first sight;[2] but surely none of the characters ever falls in love at first or any other sight, if by love we mean genuine affection or even a shred of selfless devotion.

The plot and thematic development of each story force us to conclude that the bitter, painful, humiliating thing that the characters substitute for love serves only to make more wretched their already miserable lives. In each story we encounter a character enveloped in loneliness. The character experiences some brief sexual fling with another—which seems to raise him momentarily above his condition—only to see the hollow heart of the affair at the end. If love appears in the stories in any form, it is only an inferred ideal which casts a mocking light on the characters and their sordid lives. Thus, disillusionment and bitter irony represent the major chords in the novellas' tone.

"Dulcima," the first novella in the collection, painfully demonstrates the failure of passion—or whatever it is that these characters take for love. Dulcima is the fat, ugly daughter of a family who live in squalid poverty. She blames her ugliness on the endless drudgery of helping her mother raise ten children. All about Dulcima range the results of loveless sex: ten poor children whose fanciful names—Rowena, Chalice, Cassandra, and so forth—represent a mother's attempt to reclaim some vestige of romance.

Dulcima's chance for escape comes when she begins to work for Mr. Parker, a dull, aging man whose only emotions are avarice and lechery. Dulcima's emotions are harder to analyze. Parker's lust is the first attraction of any sort that a man has felt for her, and she is vaguely thrilled; but to suggest that she feels the slightest warmth for the disgusting old man would be a distortion. Rather, she leads him on in order to "milk" him financially. "I'll pay . . . I'll pay," is his constant mating call; their first "love making" has all the warmth of a corporate merger.

Dulcima discovers just how sorry her life with Parker is when she encounters a shy young gamekeeper. She is so infatuated that she buys new clothes and has her hair done, and both she and the gamekeeper are amazed at her transformation. The relationship between the two is obviously leading to something more wholesome than her "arrangement" with Parker, but her past sins come back to haunt her. Parker sees them embracing in the woods, then tries to kill Dulcima back at his house. When Dulcima manages to evade him and locks herself in her room, Parker lies in wait outside. When the gamekeeper comes to the house the next morning, Parker shoots him dead.

Although the climax of "Dulcima" is violent, it hardly surprises us. Rather, the thematic movement and tone of the story lead to an overwhelming feeling of inevitable doom. The context of Dulcima's life— loneliness, spiritless copulation, squalor, greed, self-interest—is such that any possibility of rising above it is denied out of hand. Even the one hint of something finer—her inchoate relationship with the gamekeeper—serves only to underscore the abysmal emptiness of her past, her present, and her future.

"The Grass God" lacks the violence and spectacular squalor of "Dulcima," yet it offers us no more hope. The "grass god" is Fitzgerald, a wealthy landowner who is a bit more likable than Dulcima's Parker, but only a bit. His wealth and manners fail to conceal the fact that he is parsimonious and lecherous. We see his parsimony in his brutal and unfeeling refusal to better the living conditions of Medhurst, a tenant who lives with his brood in a tiny, cold cottage with no running water.

But Fitzgerald's clashes with Medhurst offer only a sidelight to the major issue: his summer-long adulterous relationship with the vibrant young Sarah Ferguson. At first we many feel somewhat sympathetic toward Fitzgerald. After all, the divine Sarah represents an understandably attractive alternative to Fitzgerald's nagging, unkempt wife, Cordelia. The more we see of Fitzgerald, however, the more we understand how his wife could have degenerated so over the years. Their marriage had lacked the slightest warmth: "For a very long time, he thought, there had never been any question of love."[3] Still, Cordelia's grief when she finally gives up the struggle and moves away show that some remnant of affection remained in her heart. On the other hand, Fitzgerald's perplexity at her grief demonstrates that he is incapable of understanding love or sorrow at the loss of love: "Women cried for the oddest things—sometimes for pleasure; but mostly you never knew why" (164).

If we imagine that Fitzgerald's affair with Sarah represents the appearance of genuine romance or passion in his life, we have mistaken his essentially cold-blooded, loveless nature. As he caresses her, his thoughts are not of true love but of a pleasant affair "without responsibility" (133). In the back of his mind lurks the thought that he might use the affair as a lever to force Cordelia to grant him a divorce. Indeed, not once during the hot summer of their affair does the word "love" intrude between them.

Sarah has not been fooled by Fitzgerald from the first. All along her attitude toward him—even in the act of love—is slightly cool, slightly mocking. She is something that he can have for free, she tells him, instinctively putting their relationship in terms that he best understands. She invests no genuine emotion in their relationship, apparently realizing that her investment would yield no return. Fitzgerald, after all, is an emotional bankrupt.

The end of the affair comes quickly. Sarah appears less than thrilled with the news that Cordelia has moved out. Fitzgerald avows that he loves her, but she makes it quite clear that she does not love him. The summer is over and they have had their "fun" and that is that. She rejects all his offers coolly, mockingly, and he is left with the shattering conclusion that he has absolutely nothing that she wants. Earlier he had been her "grass god"—the owner of vast pasture lands; but now we see him for the grass god that he really is: empty, heartless, powerless, a being at whose feet no one will ever fall in love or reverence.

In "The Delicate Nature" the setting shifts from England to Malaysia, but the theme remains the same. The influence of W. Somerset Maugham—to whom *The Nature of Love* is dedicated—is seen in the polished style, careful construction, and tropical setting, but Conrad's influence is even more apparent. Simpson—young and naive, traveling into the dark heart of Malaysia's jungle to a rubber plantation—is Bates's Marlow. Malan—powerful, mysterious, something not altogether right about him—is Bates's Kurtz.

But Conrad's theme of abusive power and corruption is only a resonance here. Instead, Bates explores the sordidness of lust and the pain of love that remains forever an illusion.

Simpson arrives at the rubber plantation and immediately begins hearing reports about the mysterious and intimidating Malan. The person with the "delicate nature" is Vera, Malan's fiancée. Soon the two return as husband and wife, but Vera is not the woman Simpson imagined. Rather than being a person of delicate nature, Vera is vibrant and impetuous. Still, all is not well with their marriage. Malan leaves on unaccountable journeys in the middle of the night, and Vera becomes restless. One night Vera and Simpson talk, kiss, and then make love. From then on the two meet almost nightly for wild, lusty bed-sessions. During the day Vera beguiles Simpson with smoldering, passionate stares, which, curiously, she also turns on Malan. Soon the reader senses what Simpson is too naive to see: Vera's true interest lies with her husband.

Vera and Simpson's trysts become more and more open, and Simpson fears being caught in the act. Obviously, Vera wants Malan to find out, wants to make him jealous, but Malan goes blithely on his mysterious way. We infer that his night journeys are visits to a Malay girl, and our suspicions are verified when the girl's husband kills Malan.

Simpson—naive to the last—observes that he and Vera will now be free to be together, but Vera explodes, "Who wants to be free?" (234). Then she screams out the truth to Simpson, that she had come to the plantation—against Malan's wishes—to try to win him back from the Malay girl. In effect, Simpson has been cuckolded by his mistress's husband, and we begin to learn something of the painful nature of love.

The last section of the story is anticlimactic, merely adding another level of bitterness and disillusionment to an already bleak vision. Simpson escorts Vera back down the river toward civilization and uses the opportunity to press her further with his love. When he tells her that he cannot live without her, she coldly replies, "You know now how it feels" (240). "It" is love, and love for Simpson, Vera, and all the characters in these bitter novellas is a painful thing indeed.

Summer in Salandar (1957)

Bates's next collection of novellas—*Summer in Salandar* (1957)—was published only four years after *The Nature of Love*, and in many ways it is a thematic extension of its predecessor. All the novellas deal with love relationships, and all end unhappily. In *The Nature of Love*, however, love most often translates into degrading lust; in the present collection we occasionally encounter relationships that—had conditions been happier—might have developed into something resembling a healthy love. Another major difference in the collections is in their respective tones. The novellas in *The Nature of Love* envelop the reader in a suffocating fog of gloom, whereas in two of the *Summer in Salandar* selections we are refreshed with an occasional ray of humor.

In general, reviewers are much happier with *Summer in Salandar* than with *The Nature of Love*. Most find Bates's key to success in his masterful characterization and unblemished prose style. Although a few reviewers remain unconvinced, some are so extravagant in their praise that we must once again wonder why Bates's reputation among contemporary scholars and readers is so tenuous.

The opening story—"Death of a Huntsman"—may seem to contradict our earlier observation that the collection displays a greater variety of tones than *The Nature of Love*. We begin the story in gloom and the tone never noticeably brightens thereafter. Indeed, the title tells us more, perhaps, than we want to know.

We meet the protagonist—Harry Barnfield— on the commuter train returning from London to his country home. Harried, a little dowdy, late middle-aged, Harry presents an easy target for his fellow travelers' jibes. Arriving home to be greeted by a nagging, alcoholic wife affords little solace. But one day Harry encounters Valerie Whittington riding across his land. She is nineteen and vivacious, but wretchedly lonely living in the country with her mother. As it happens, her mother, Edna, is an old "friend" of Harry's. They had had an affair years past, and when Harry calls on mother and daughter, it is obvious that Edna would like to rekindle the fires. Unfortunately, over the years Edna has developed into a boozy, bitchy, frowsy woman—much like Harry's wife.

Harry, of course, much prefers young Valerie, and she him. They meet in the woods again and again, but the object of their rendezvous is not simply to fulfill lustful passions. They appear honestly happy together—each the other's haven from loneliness. But it cannot last. Even if the title did not tell us as much, the tone and imagery would. The symbol for their love is a quince tree with a single, beautiful blossom but the season is autumn, and the last time they meet in the woods the quince blossom falls off. When Valerie arrives at the fateful autumn ball wearing a quince-colored dress, we know that the end is near.

At the ball, Valerie openly defies Edna, who realizes that Harry's affections are aimed not at her as she had hoped, but at her daughter. Harry sits in his car attempting to explain to Edna how much in love he and Valerie are. When Edna cruelly insists that Valerie will have to be told about their past relationship, Harry—seeing his one hope for true love about to be shattered—goes berserk and strikes Edna. He then drives wildly down the dark road. Edna jumps out, unhurt, but Harry dies in a crash.

Although the novella ends unhappily, some genuine affection between two persons was apparent, as it never was in *The Nature of Love*. Thus, although the tone of the story remains one of almost unrelieved gloom, perhaps we are beginning to see just a hint of sunshine in Bates's bleak thematic sky.

In "Night Run to the West" we again encounter two characters who attempt to break out of shells of loneliness by means of a shared passion, but fail in the end. But instead of the heavy melancholy that pervaded earlier novellas following much the same pattern, "Night Run to the West" presents a more complex tone within a structure which—if not comic—is certainly ironic.

Bates beguiles the reader by weaving an atmosphere of mystery and enchantment about a house at which Williams, a truck driver, stops to make a call one night. There he meets Francie Broderick, a woman who shares some of the mystery and "untidy, uneasy strength"[4] with the sprawling house. The next morning Williams stops off to return a borrowed tea flask, only to argue with Calvin—a crippled, petulant, wormlike man who we learn is Francie's husband.

Williams drops in to visit Francie on each of his nightly runs. At first they merely talk, but on Francie's birthday she seduces Williams, and from then on they become lovers. At this point in the story we have a traditional comic structure. Two young people fall in love—although "love" is perhaps a bit too strong a term in this case—but fail to establish a permanent relationship because of an older man, Calvin, the "blocking character" in Northrop Frye's theory of comedy.

The situation is a bit more complex, however, than this simple scheme implies. For instance, our sympathy for Francie is mitigated somewhat by the circumstances of her relationship with Calvin. Certainly, she lost her one true love in the war, but that fact makes it doubly strange that she should continue to live with Calvin, who made his fortune off a bomb fuse he invented. The truth, as she readily admits, is that Francie remains with Calvin only in order to inherit his money when he dies. Thus, if their marriage is a loveless one, conniving Francie must share a good deal of the blame.

She must share more than a good deal of the blame, as Williams learns upon rushing to Calvin's room one day when Calvin is apparently having an attack of some sort. Williams talks to Calvin and soon realizes that—instead of being a waspish, vindictive little man—Calvin is friendly, warm, and as full of as much life as his crippled body will allow. Indeed, he is much more likable than Francie, whom he loves dearly.

Our sympathies shift to Calvin even more when Williams discovers by accident that the whiskey and sleeping pills that he has been giving Calvin—at Francie's suggestion—form a potentially deadly combination. Williams rushes to the house, only to find Calvin in the best of spirits and health. The whiskey, he tells Williams, was just the proper stimulus for his heart. Williams decides at the moment that he wants no more of the conniving Mrs. Broderick and asks Calvin to forward a message to her. "Tell her that from now on I'll be working in the daytime" (126).

The structure of "Night Run to the West" may be broken down into two contrasting movements. The first provides false insight into the personalities of two characters (Francie and Calvin) and initiates a romance between Francie and Williams, while the second reverses our earlier estimation of Francie's and Calvin's personalities and charts the demise of the two lovers' affair. Although the three characters end approximately where they began—sadder but wiser, perhaps— we feel that the undertone of the story has been comic, not tragic.

The tone of "Summer in Salandar" is decidedly more pathetic, yet the movement/countermovement structure is much like that of "Night Run to the West." The novella is an appropriate form for this type of structure since its length allows Bates the time to make probable the change in personality of the major characters and the reversal of the plot's apparent movement.

The first section of "Summer in Salandar" introduces us to Manson, an Englishman who works for a shipping line. He is miserably bored with the few passengers of the even fewer ships that venture to the oppressively hot harbor—bored with Salandar, bored with his life. The mood for the entire novella is set in the first section as Manson listlessly watches a passing funeral procession. At the end of the section he leaves to greet one more ship as "the last black beetle of the funeral cortege flashes past him, expensively glittering, lurching dangerously, chasing the dead: a car filled with weeping men" (132). But the ship that he greets offers a surprising passenger: Vane, a saucy, pretty, vivacious young woman.

Vane bullies Manson into showing her the few sights that Salandar possesses, and he is obviously disconcerted by this lively young girl, who represents something of a threat to his listless, cynical passivity.

Thus, the first movement is established. Simply because the two are thrown together with so few alternatives, we imagine, a romance *must* develop; and, as is usual in such cases, the life-affirming woman will reinvigorate the life-denying man. No sooner does Bates lull us into expecting the tried-and-true formula, however, than the contrasting second movement begins to undercut the first.

Characterization and plot movement begin to invert themselves at the very moment that they seem to be reaching their logical conclusion.

Vane bullies the reluctant Manson into taking her on a trek into the scorching-hot hills. Gradually, Manson becomes enamored of the young lady, and—partly to escape the irritatingly smug servant Manuel—he insists that the two go on alone to the serra plateau. His goal itself is a significant foreshadowing, since the Indians avoid the serra plateau because of its loneliness. But just when Manson begins to assume some of Vane's adventuresomeness, she becomes more passive and constantly lags behind. Her response to his advances is hardly passionate, and her *joie de vivre* dissolves as she admits that her life has been "a sort of hell" (180).

At this point, then, the two major characters have reversed their personalities. Manson is active, aggressive, eager for romance while Vane has become listless and pessimistic. Any thoughts of romance disappear when Vane perversely sends Manson back down a long, steep trail to fetch her bag. Dazed by the heat and his anger and frustration, Manson falls and injures his foot. The novella ends with a delirious Manson shouting and fighting the men who bear him back to the city. But he is ignored as they march on with all the slow solemnity of a funeral procession.

"The Queen of Spain Fritillary" is the weakest novella in the collection. Seventeen-year-old Laura flirts with eccentric Frederick Fielding-Brown until the enraptured sixty-year-old proposes. She turns down his proposal but continues to visit him and keeps his hopes alive. Unfortunately, Mrs. Carfax, who had been Frederick's close friend for years, makes a scene and then, humiliated, commits suicide.

Tone and atmosphere—which elsewhere, particularly in "Summer in Salandar," represents Bates's strength—fail him here. The narrator of the story is Laura, an aging woman looking back on one summer in her youth. The tone early in the story is light, offhanded, sarcastic—appropriate enough if the events concern youth's common foibles—and in the end is wistful and nostalgic—again, appropriate if the narrator is recalling events with some fondness. But surely neither tone suits a story that climaxes with the suicide of a lonely, abused, humiliated woman.

The Grapes of Paradise: Four Short Novels (1960)

The Grapes of Paradise: Four Short Novels (published in England as *An Aspidistra in Babylon*, 1960) continues Bates's analysis of not the nature of love but the nature of bad love: frustrated love, painful love, joyless love, love that ends in violence. Each novella offers a variation on the traditional love triangle, with one or more of the participants blinded by passion to the reality of the situation. Only one offers even a hint of hope in the end.

The first novella—"An Aspidistra in Babylon"—concerns a teenage girl, Christine, who allows herself to be seduced by Major Blaine, a suave but conscienceless wastrel who desires money more than he desires Christine. In her gullibility she offers to steal money from Blaine's aunt but is caught in the act by the maid, Ruby, who blithely laughs it off. Christine waits all night for Blaine to appear to claim her and the money, but Ruby comes back instead after a night on the town—and in bed— with none other than Christine's beloved Blaine.

The problem that appeared in "The Queen of Spain Fritillary"—distracting tone—again plagues "An Aspidistra in Babylon." The story is narrated by an aging Christine, who looks back with smug superiority at her younger self. Unfortunately, she evinces so much scorn for the teenage Christine that the reader can hardly take her, or the story, seriously. For instance, after a particularly saccharine compliment from Blaine, the narrator sarcastically recalls, "Could any girl, I ask you, want more than that? I lapped up these blandishments as a kitten laps up warm new milk."[5] Later, after another of Blaine's sweet persuasions, the narrator concludes, "Stupid though this no doubt sounds it was heaven for me to hear him talk like that" (37). In his better works Bates allows the reader to decide if such things are "stupid"; here he insists upon interpreting everything for us, and his efforts result in diminishing returns.

Bates is more effective when he employs a narrator who does not have a personal stake in the events of the story and does not have total knowledge of the circumstances of events. This allows the reader to join the narrator in the process of discovery.

Such is the technique in "A Prospect of Orchards," and the result is a convincing work. Here the narrator merely observes and is not personally involved in the central action of the story. The narrator meets shy, awkward Arthur Templeton—the personification of ineffectuality—on a train, and the conversation turns to Arthur's pet project—attempting to grow an apple with the taste and characteristics of a pear. This utterly pointless and farfetched notion perfectly captures Arthur's inability to comprehend and deal with life's realities.

When the narrator drops by Arthur's estate for a visit, he finds a houseful of snobbish, supercilious guests—friends of Arthur's randy wife, Valerie. Arthur himself has been relegated to the barn. The narrator spends the majority of his visit fending off Valerie's open advances. On a later visit—for Valerie's birthday party—the narrator finds that Arthur has been allowed into the house, but as little more than a harried and much-abused lackey. Arthur divides his time between waiting on Valerie and young, bored Anthea Barlow. On the narrator's last visit, he learns that Valerie has gone on a vacation with an admirer and Arthur is having an affair with Anthea.

The realization that Arthur, too, is having an affair only intensifies our feeling that he is a lonely, cowardly man living in a morally bankrupt world. This is the type of situation and character with which Bates has dealt so well in the past, and "A Prospect of Orchards" is one more example of his deft, sensitive touch.

Most reviewers judge "The Grapes of Paradise" to be the best novella in the collection. Bates splashes his canvas with rich, vivid hues—appropriate for this tale of clashing passions in sultry Tahiti.

Once again we find an older narrator, Henry, looking back on past action, but this time the tone reflects all the regret and pathos we would expect considering the tragic, violent events. Henry does not inspire our admiration. Always taking, never giving, he is the epitome of self-interest. Yet the crucial event in the story turns on an innocent act of tenderness: Henry kisses the massive, spectacularly ugly native girl Thérèsa. Thereafter she worships him with a consuming, jealous, possessive love.

When Henry later begins to sleep with a petite, refined, half-Chinese girl—the perfect foil for "dark, powerful, and magnificent" (212) Thérèsa—the stage is set for the violent conclusion. While out on a boat fishing with Henry and her brother, Timi, Thérèsa explodes in jealous fury and slashes Henry with a knife. When Timi falls overboard, she dives in and tosses him back into the boat; but before she can climb back in a shark attacks her and she loses a leg. Timi pilots the boat back as Thérèsa and Henry lie in each others' arms in a spreading pool of blood. As they approach the shore, Henry sees that she is dead. But Bates spares us the maudlin ending. Thérèsa—described elsewhere as resembling an idol in her great strength—"seemed to be glaring back at the flaming sky, handsome and almost contemptuous as she lay there . . . and all across the lagoon the crowing of jungle cocks was proud and clear" (239).

Neither the theme nor the characterization in "The Grapes of Paradise" is profound; rather, the novella relies upon the elemental conflict of love and hate, serenity and violence for its appeal. As is the case with any fine storyteller, Bates holds us enchanted until the end.

"A Month by the Lake" offers the only hint of optimism in the collection. Even the relative happiness in the end, however, comes only after much pain and humiliation. As we saw earlier in "An Aspidistra in Babylon," and to a degree in the other two novellas, the problems result from the characters' inability to distinguish truth from illusion.

At the beginning of the story Major Wilshaw—vacationing one summer on a Swiss lake—is blind to the fact that Miss Bently has fallen in love with him. Instead, he reserves his affections for young, flightly, obnoxiously egotistical Miss Beaumont. He soon learns the error of his ways, but Miss Bently fails to see that he has begun to turn his gaze upon a more receptive target—herself. To make him jealous, which is no longer necessary, she takes up with a young, opportunistic Italian—a social impropriety, to say the least.

Thus both Major Wilshaw and Miss Bently, blinded by vanity and jealousy, are bound to play the fool, and the remainder of the novella is a bitter comedy of errors. The end finds the two, having lost their young lovers, together at last, apparently prepared to share a new life. The optimistic ending is not forced or manipulated but is an earned vision: their new wisdom purchased at the price of suffering and humiliation. Although it lacks the exotic spectacle of "Summer in Salander" or "The Grapes of Paradise," "A Month by the Lake" remains one of Bates's most sensitive novellas.

The Golden Oriole (1962)

The reviews of Bates's next volume of novellas—*The Golden Oriole*—are almost equally divided between the favorable and the unfavorable, an appropriate dichotomy for such an inconsistent collection. The tones of the novellas range from the bleak to the dreamlike to the low comic to the farcical. Varied tone affords a pleasing change of pace, but unfortunately the quality is equally varied.

The title novella, "The Golden Oriole," is probably the most interesting offering in the collection. The dreamlike ambience reminds one of "Alexander" and several other of Bates's stories about youth. Although the three major characters are all middle-aged, the comparison to "Alexander" is not inappropriate; for the protagonist, Prinny (Princess), is a forty-year-old child. She spends her days playing hide-and-seek with her husband, Mansfield. Their house sits in an idyllic country setting, surrounded by gardens and orchards, and into this Eden, apparently, no pain or sin or conflict of any kind enters.

Fiction abhors innocence as much as nature does a vacuum, and we know that the situation cannot continue. George Seamark comes to see Mansfield about business and instead finds Prinny hiding in an apple tree. They talk and then meet the following day. Her strong and sudden attraction to his solid, virile earthiness suggests that something has been missing in her marriage. Obviously, her husband has been so intent on keeping her a child that he has forgotten that she is his wife. We receive many indications, in fact, that their marriage has never been consummated. The two sleep in separate bedrooms—a fact that Prinny can disclose only with much confusion and embarrassment. Her bare shoulders and arms have an "extraordinary pristine smoothness. . . . It was not merely unblemished; it gave the impression of never having been touched before."[6] When George asks her to remove her clothes, she is outraged: she had never done that before. Later, when he touches her breasts, we learn that no one had done that before either.

"The Golden Oriole" is a story of discovery: a woman's discovery of a dormant instinct for sex and love. Concealment and discovery form a recurring motif throughout. Prinny and her husband play hide-and-seek of course; but also, after George surprises Prinny with a kiss, she runs and hides in confusion. When he finds and tries to seduce her, she says that she will do what he asks, but the seduction must not be deliberate; it must be "a discovery." Thus, when she wanders outside that night, George surprises her, and she "let him make his discovery" (123) under the same apple tree in which he had first found her hiding.

Prinny's final discovery is a more somber one. George had been away for some months on business when Mansfield brings home the news that George was accidentally killed on the ship back to England. Prinny runs outside at the news and stares wildly about her: "It was as if she had found herself suddenly naked and had no way of hiding any longer" (125). Thus, after discovering that the fantasy world of her marriage suffers in comparison to true passion, Prinny also discovers a more bitter truth: no Eden exists to insulate us from the harsh world of reality.

Less successful than "The Golden Oriole" are "The Ring of Truth," "The Quiet Girl," and "Mr. Featherstone Takes a Ride." The problem with "The Ring of Truth"—the story of a young man stimulated by a dream to seek out a distant hotel where he meets his father's former confidante—is, as several reviewers have noted, that it lacks the ring of truth.

"The Quiet Girl" tells the story of a woman who spent her youth and most of her adult years in an impenetrable shell of isolation. Even when she takes on a series of lovers, each one serves only to drive her farther into herself. Only when she meets a lively, lusty traveling salesman does she begin to break out of her cocoon of isolation; but he blithely moves on, leaving her "for ever listening to the echo of voices" (94). The "Quiet

Girl" is an interesting character study, but it fails to meet Bates's usual level due to his insistence on interpreting the psychological impact of each event. At his best, the action sufficiently dramatizes theme and characterization so that no explanation is necessary.

"Mr. Featherstone Takes a Ride" follows the traditional motif—particularly popular in American local color—of the "city slicker" being duped by the "country bumpkin." In this case the city slicker is Mr. Featherstone—a green, priggish philosophy student on recess from the Ivory Tower—who hitches a ride from fun-loving, opportunistic Niggler. Niggler properly shocks and dismays Featherstone with his lusty, amoral ways and in the end dupes him out of five pounds. This is the type of thing that Bates does with great relish throughout the Pop Larkin series, and readers find it greatly entertaining or merely infantile. There seems to be no middle ground.

The low comedy of "Mr. Featherstone Takes a Ride" is followed by the hilarious farce of "The World Is Too Much With Us." Indeed, "The World Is Too Much With Us" might very well be seen as Bates's parody of his own novellas. Once more we find the love triangle with at least one of the participants blind to the true state of affairs. As is so often the case, passion turns to jealousy and breaks out into ugly violence. In the end one of the participants is coldly cast aside.

This love triangle, however, hardly qualifies as a traditional one for the simple reason that Mr. Plomley's first true love—whom he cruelly jilts for orange-haired, big-bosomed Phoebe Spencer—is a hen. Georgina the hen lives in smug complacency with Plomley until Phoebe intrudes. To be fair to Plomley, he does try to tell Phoebe about Georgina, omitting only that she is a hen. He explains that Georgina rarely presents herself due to shyness—"She broods" (191).

Georgina does indeed brood and sulk. Plomley attempts to appease her by giving her whiskey in a pen-filler—her favorite treat—and tearfully apologizes for his attentions to Phoebe. But the final straw comes when he moves his darling from her quarters in his house to the potting shed. He promises to visit often, but she flies (literally) into a jealous rage and bites him on the ear. Plomley pins her down and threatens to "wring your damn neck," and she glares back as if to say, "Go on, hit me you great brute. You've got me down now, haven't you? Hit me" (200).

Plomley decides to wash his hands of Georgina. He goes to Phoebe and tells her that he is through with Georgina forever and intimates that there was someone before Georgina. Obviously, concludes sympathetic Phoebe, the "slut" caught him on the rebound. The last scene of the story occurs sometime in the future. Plomley and Phoebe lie beside each other in bed, married now, and Plomley gives her whiskey in a penfiller. She lays beside him "with all the broody contentment of a hen about to lay an egg" (204). "The World Is Too Much With Us" concludes the collection. By this time Bates had published four collections of novellas—not to mention numerous short stories and novels—in nine years, nearly all constructed around some variation on the love triangle. It would be merely conjecture to say that Bates was beginning to tire of the form. But "The World Is Too Much With Us" certainly offers a delightful, hilarious parody of passion, wandering affections, jealousy, betrayal, violence, and new love: all elements in the traditional love triangle.

The Four Beauties (1968)

If the parody of "The World Is Too Much With Us" suggests that Bates had begun to tire of the love triangle as a subject for his novellas, the following six years apparently afforded sufficient respite to allow him to return to the conflict with renewed vigor. After that six-year interval, in 1968, Bates published his final collection of novellas, *The Four Beauties*, two of which explore love triangles of sorts.

The two novellas which do not are less interesting, but not for that reason. "The Chords of Youth" suffers from a lack of focus. The first part of the story centers on the foibles of trying to recapture youth, while the second half introduces the theme of nationalism. Bates never satisfactorily integrates the two themes. Actually, plot and theme in "The Chords of Youth" merely provide an excuse for introducing a group of eccentric, comic characters. We have great fun with these walking caricatures for a time, but the lack of focus eventually results in tedium.

"The White Wind" is a good yarn—except that it amounts to little more than *The Cruise of the Breadwinner* shifted to the South Seas. Once again we read of a naive young boy who goes to sea, encounters shocking violence and death, and returns with a matured vision. Reviewers who lament that in the later years Bates has nothing new to offer could well use "The White Wind" as evidence.

On the other hand, one could rebut this view by pointing to the remaining two novellas—"The Four Beauties" and "The Simple Life." Although both offer variations on the love triangle, the treatment is fresh and the writing as masterful as ever.

In "The Four Beauties" Bates expands the traditional love triangle into an affair with five participants. But the sordidness and violence that marked most of the earlier novellas is replaced here by that rarefied, dreamlike ambience which Bates has employed so effectively in the past. The story concerns the narrator, who frequents a café run by shabby Mrs. Davenport and her three daughters, all beauties and all full of gaiety—"so much so that I constantly felt that the little café would one day explode, evaporate into thin celestial air and, with its three beauties and their mother, vanish forever."[7]

The three daughters, as it turns out, do in effect vanish into thin air, but only after the narrator has had an affair with each in her turn. Such a situation would undoubtedly lead to much unpleasantness in most of Bates's works, but mild jealousy is the strongest emotion exhibited by any of the daughters. In fact, rather than censuring the inconstant narrator we feel that he is little more than a plaything of girls—the oldest only eighteen—whose wiles are as ancient as Eve. Indeed, he suffers for his inconstancy more than the daughters. "In the presence of one," he laments, "I would be haunted by the absence of another" (47).

Just when the narrator's affairs with the three become the most tangled, their mother sells the café and moves to a distant part of the country with her daughters. It is many years later before he accidentally meets Mrs. Davenport again. Two of her daughters have moved away and one has drowned while swimming. But this news interests the narrator less than does Mrs. Davenport herself. She looks rejuvenated from her shabby, unkempt appearance. Too, she wears her hair in the style of one daughter, the dress of another, and the pearl necklace of the third. "It's very, very nice to see you," she purrs. "The girls were not the only ones in the family who always liked you" (86). We know that he once more is about to fall under the enchanting spell of one of the four beauties.

"The Simple Life" explores the same sort of sordid, painful love triangle that has attracted Bates so often. Although it hardly differs in kind from earlier efforts, its general excellence makes it particularly worthwhile reading.

The simple life is what Bartholomew seeks at his seaside cottage with his wife, Stella. Stella, in turn, hates the simple life or any other kind of life, apparently, with a consuming passion. Lazy, alcoholic, unkempt, thirty-five but looking fifty-five, Stella gazes at a landscape which others might view as untrammeled and sees only "three withered willows sticking nakedly up from the water, like grey arms caught and fossiled in the act of drowning" (7). Her life-denying pessimism is evident in the first sentence of the story: "Winter began in August; or so it always seemed to her" (7).

Their marriage consists entirely of bickering, insults, and abuse. The possibility of some joy enters Stella's life, however, with the appearance of Roger Blackburn, seventeen, who does odd jobs about the cottage. Appropriately enough for the nature-loving Bates, Stella first shows signs of life when Roger points out a skylark to her. She claims never to have seen one before and enthuses, "It's the most beautiful thing in the world" (17).

Stella and Roger's affair begins in earnest when she remains at the cottage while Bartholomew returns to the city. One could hardly say, however, that love is the motivating force. In fact, Roger first "seduces" Stella after she passes out in a drunken stupor. The endearments that encouraged Roger were nothing more than the "darlings" and "dears" with which Stella habitually punctuated her speech. The next morning Stella actually has to ask if a seduction occurred, and when she learns that it did, she brutally informs him that he was not very successful. It is one measure of her insensitivity that she does not even realize that she has hurt the boy's feelings.

Spring comes with its "impassioned ceaseless song of skylarks" (27), and the affair continues, but Stella becomes a trifle bored with Roger. She shows little interest in love or tenderness but demands thrills and excitement. One day for an extra thrill she lies naked in the sun waiting for Roger; but the wait lasts hours as a fog—announced by the "slow funereal boom of a fog-horn" (29)—ominously blots out the sun. When Roger finally does arrive, it is only to tell her that he is breaking off their affair. "I don't think it's fair to Mr. Bartholomew" (32), he reasons.

In fact, Roger's interest turns decidedly toward the husband. Bartholomew buys a boat and, with Roger's help, repairs it and plans a cruise around France. When Bartholomew admits to becoming "sort of attached to him [Roger]," Stella sneers that he has found a "pretty boy" and hopes that they enjoy their "honeymoon" while she "stayed at home and burnt her bloody heart out" (37). The two men do leave on their cruise, and if Stella does not literally burn her heart out, it is only because her heart was only a cold cinder with little combustible matter from the beginning. The story ends in a image of loneliness, cruelty, and death—". . . ahead of her a heron rose from the dykes in slow flight, a grey ghost watching for prey" (38)—as Stella contemplates the same desolate landscape that so depressed her in the beginning.

Bates combines cruelly accurate characterization, striking imagery, and dialogue alive with exacerbating bitterness to make "The Simple Life" one of his most devastating comments on contemporary relationships. The novella is circular in structure, journeying only from desolation to desolation, yet in doing so it lays bare the soul of a very nearly soulless woman who, trapped in a loveless marriage, loses her clumsy lover to her own husband.

The Triple Echo (1970)

The Triple Echo is Bates's last novella, and it shares with *The Cruise of the Breadwinner* (1946) the distinction of being his most fully realized. The fact that the work took twenty-five years to complete shows the energies that Bates devoted to it.[8] In this novella of love and death, war and embattled peace, Bates skillfully blends plot, characterization, atmosphere, and image into an organic whole. Moreover, whereas in many of his works in the later period Bates exhibits an inclination to make emphatically a thematic point (not always to the detriment of the story, certainly), *The Triple Echo* is strikingly evocative, as reverberating in its implications as its title suggests. Indeed, several of Bates thematic concerns come to a head in his last novella: the devastating effects of war, the forbidding prospect of a life of loneliness, the destructiveness of suffocating passions.

War's impact on all concerned is established in the novella's opening passage. "My husband's a prisoner with the Japs," states Mrs. Charlesworth. "I'll probably never see him again. That's all I know."[9] Mrs. Charlesworth lives on a secluded farm in rural England, apparently as far removed from the war as one could be, but war intrudes in her thoughts of her husband, and its effects are seen in the sorry condition of the farm itself—in a progressive state of decay since her husband's absence.

Worse, with her husband gone and her farm "cut off from the main road" (7), Mrs. Charlesworth is almost totally isolated from humanity. Ironically, instead of being peacefully locked away from the war, she reacts to her isolation like an embattled soldier. She constantly carries a shotgun on her rounds of errands, shoots her injured dog, shoots at invading rats and foxes, and guards against people "nicking things" (8). We might judge the young woman to be hardy and self-reliant, yet Bates makes it clear that her situation is desperate. Her eyes "had something of the lost glassiness seen in the eyes of birds imprisoned in cases, with only dead grass and ferns for company" (8).

The image of Mrs. Charlesworth being an imprisoned bird initiates a pattern of bird imagery throughout the first section of the story. Birds, particularly nightingales and skylarks, frequently appear in Bates's fiction as symbols for the liberated spirit (thus, the skylarks in "The Simple Life"); significantly, when young soldier Barton intrudes upon

Mrs. Charlesworth's isolation, he is enthralled by a nightingale's song, but she is oblivious. As the first section progresses, she begins to be attracted to the shy young man and realizes how much she has missed human contact. By the end of the section both listen attentively to the nightingale's song.

Barton is on leave from the nearby army camp, and he despises the military with bitter intensity: "God, how I loathe it. The army, I mean. God how I hate it" (17). A farmboy before being drafted, Barton is drawn to Mrs. Charlesworth's farm by the land as much as by Mrs. Charlesworth herself: "He'd be better off on the land. Growing something. That's where he belonged" (14).

Barton returns again and again to do odd jobs for Mrs. Charlesworth, but as his leave nears its end it is obvious that their relationship will take a romantic turn. The scene of what was to be Barton's last visit to the farm represents Bates at his best. A storm approaches on the hot, sultry afternoon, and nature abounds in images of tension, impending conflict: "Toward the west, half way across the valley, two clouds like smoky mushrooms were slowly being drawn to each other, fusing into a single ominous thundery mass that shut out the sun" (20). The suffocating, destructive power of the passion that will later appear is perfectly foreshadowed by the imagery throughout the scene.

Mrs. Charlesworth invites Barton to spend the night, and they begin to feel themselves "sort of in a vacuum. You're just two people and you're here and nothing outside matters. There isn't anybody else. There isn't any war" (26). Of course, there is a war, and Mrs. Charlesworth feels that she is skirting too near it when Barton announces that he is never going back to the army, that he is going to live on with her. That Barton has made a decision in accordance with nature as opposed to civilization and its wars is emphasized by the reappearance of the nightingale. At the moment of his decision, "Far above, in the darkening beeches, a nightingale started a burst of song, faded into silence, and then emerged again in a long triumphant trill" (33).

Mrs. Charlesworth finally agrees to let Barton stay, but to prevent discovery she makes him wear a dress, a padded bra, and lipstick. He becomes "Jill." Changes in wearing apparel are significant throughout *The Triple Echo*. It is when Barton changes from his uniform to civilian clothes that Mrs. Charlesworth becomes sexually attracted to him. In the same way, when she dons a skirt and blouse after wearing work clothes, Barton shows an interest in her. But the morning after he first spends the night, he puts on his uniform again, and their relationship becomes strained.

Thus, when Barton wears woman's clothes for weeks on end and allows his hair to grow long, Mrs. Charlesworth begins to think of him as a woman. Her love for Barton has a suffocating intensity, while at the same time she resents having the responsibility of head of the household placed on her shoulders. As a result, she alternately fawns over him and explodes in vituperation. In one bitter scene she calls him "kept," and true to form "Jill" nearly weeps in humiliation.

As Mrs. Charlesworth and Barton's domestic troubles deepen, the war is never far away. One day a subaltern and sergeant come to the farm trying to locate an old road for army maneuvers. The reentrance of the army into their secluded lives is signaled by images of war. The snow is "flying white bullets against black yews," while the trees form a "rampart of beeches" (44). The two army men soon leave, but only after the sergeant crudely flirts with Mrs. Charlesworth and, when repulsed, threatens to turn his attentions to her "sister," Jill.

The sergeant and subaltern return again and again, despite Mrs. Charlesworth's open hostility. She keeps careful vigil, but Barton takes the whole matter as a great joke. Then one day Mrs. Charlesworth returns from a shopping trip only to find the sergeant and "Jill" conversing. After the sergeant leaves, she finds that "Jill" has accepted an invitation to the Christmas dance. Mrs. Charlesworth is beside herself with rage and horror; she calls Barton a "woman" and he calls her a "bitch."

Over the following days they drop the matter, but when Christmas Eve arrives Mrs. Charlesworth is amazed to find that Barton actually intends to go through with his date. Obviously, her love has become so suffocating that an evening away from her justifies the danger of discovery. When the sergeant leaves with Barton—radiant in his dress, long hair, and fair skin—Mrs. Charlesworth is stunned with fear, anger, but also a "stiffened somber jealousy" (70).

Despite her fears, Barton returns safely from the dance, and by the day after Christmas snow has fallen, and Mrs. Charlesworth once more feels isolated and safe. Just as she begins to make amends to Barton, however, a jeep approaches carrying military policemen, among them the sergeant. Barton runs off to hide in the woods as Mrs. Charlesworth tries to distract the sergeant with taunts. But the sergeant spots Barton and gives chase, hurling back a taunt: "husband a prisoner with the Japs, too my God" (79). When the sergeant marches back to the house leading a handcuffed Barton, Mrs. Charlesworth calmly raises her shotgun and shoots them both. The blast echoes three times.

The Triple Echo is a story of echoes and reverberations: the lost husband—perhaps the most pitiful victim of all—who intrudes only at the beginning and end of the novella; the passions which arise out of the vacuum of Mrs. Charlesworth's isolation only to reverberate with expanding consequences throughout the story; the hints of homosexuality and lesbianism—subtle but disturbing echoes behind the interplay of mannish woman and womanish man; and most important, the war which crashes and roars in the world at large and echoes throughout Mrs. Charlesworth's isolated life. And in the end the war enlists her in its ancient routine of violence, blood, and death.

The Triple Echo is the richest of Bates's novellas—one that the reader can return to with great rewards—and it represents a fitting climax to his fiction career.

Chapter Nine
H. E. Bates's Career in Retrospect

Recent "Masterpiece Theatre" adaptations of some of Bates's works, televised in Britain and the United States, have sparked increased interest in Bates and his fiction. While the renewed interest is modest—nothing like a "Renaissance" of Bates scholarship is evident—it does suggest that history might indeed be kind to Bates. Bates's reputation was at its lowest ebb in the final two decades of his writing career, and it is this nadir of estimation that has colored critical thinking about his work. To what degree is this lowered estimation justified? To what degree does it distort his true contribution to English literature? What, finally, is Bates's place among his contemporaries in the twentieth century?

The decline in Bates's reputation is not hard to trace. It began after World War II with his novels of the Far East: works with exotic locales and much sex and violence but shallow characterization. Two novels written in the mid-1950s, *Love for Lydia* and *The Feast of July*, were finer works, yet many critics, even in generally praising Bates, moaned that he had nothing new to say. This "nothing new to say" becomes the *idée fixe* of reviewers in the later years of Bates's career, with justification. Bates was, after all, a professional writer, with the emphasis on "professional." His autobiography reveals an almost obsessive zeal to earn his living as a writer, and for Bates this meant a book or two a year. Repetition to the point of staleness was impossible to avoid totally, and it is in the later years that redundancy plagues Bates the most. The Larkin novels represented a welcome departure to some reviewers, a deplorable lapse of taste to others. Even those who liked the Larkin series found them richly diverting but hardly serious literary efforts.

Thus far we have mentioned only Bates's novels in the later years. His short stories and novellas during that same period were often the equal of his finest efforts of the 1920s and 1930s. But literary history has shown as a general rule that when an author writes both novels and short fiction, it is the novels that largely determine his reputation. Consciously or subconsciously, to many critics a writer "comes of age" when he begins to publish novels. And although Bates did indeed publish a number of fine novels, novels that deserve reevaluation, his novelistic skills never matched those that he brought to short fiction.

In fact, his strengths as a short-story writer were often liabilities in longer works. He could quickly and economically sketch a believable and interesting character in a short story, for instance, but over the course of a novel too often the characters remained merely sketches. Too often our first encounter with a character in a Bates novel tells us virtually everything we need to know or will ever know, of a fundamental nature, about the character. Bates could capture the feel of a situation with power and intensity in a short story; but novels—at least the conventional novels that he chose to write—require progressive action, and plots were never Bates's strength or interest. Similarly, Bates's greatest strength in the short story was evoking a special atmosphere that often became more of a personality in the story than any of its characters. While this may be a virtue in the short story, too much reliance on mood or atmosphere may strangle a novel, or simply become tedious.

As a short-story writer Bates had the great luck and the great misfortune to begin his career at a time when many of the giants of the genre were at the height of their power and reputation: modern masters such as Hemingway, Anderson, Lawrence, Mansfield, and so forth. Learning from them, as well as from the acknowledged nineteenth-century masters, Bates from the very first wrote stories showing remarkable skill and craftsmanship. At his best, Bates was the equal of Mansfield and Lawrence (and he was never as bad as Lawrence's worst), and over the course of his career he was certainly a more versatile and probably a consistently better short-story writer than Sherwood Anderson. Yet Anderson, Mansfield, Lawrence, Hemingway, and Joyce were innovators, as Bates was not, so he seems doomed to remain always in their shadows.

Bates belongs in a second generation of modern English writers—along with V. S. Pritchett, William Sansom, and others—who, beginning in the 1920s and 1930s, built on the foundation laid by earlier giants and wrote both novels and short stories, although the latter are generally their strength. Bates's contribution is distinctive because it is sociological and historical as well as literary. Like Joyce, Lawrence, Faulkner, and Hardy in an earlier time, Bates captured the heart and soul of a locale and its people. Bates's Yoknapatawpha County was the

English Midlands; and his novels, novellas, and short stories of life there, especially during the decades of the late nineteenth and early twentieth centuries, comprise a rich, colorful, living tapestry. Uncle Silas, the farmers and poachers and passionate women and violent young men, the fields and meadows that he captures with a painter's skill are the best guarantee, even more than his mastery of the English language, that Bates's fiction will live on.

Notes and References

Chapter One

1. H. E. Bates, *The Vanished World: An Autobiography* (Columbia, Mo., 1969), p. 24. All future references to this work appear in the text.
2. H. E. Bates, "Thomas Hardy and Joseph Conrad," in *The English Novelists: A Survey of the Novel by Twenty Contemporary Novelists*, ed. Derek Verschoyle (London, 1936), p. 237.
3. H. E. Bates, *The Blossoming World: An Autobiography* (Columbia, Mo., 1971), p. 59.

Chapter Two

1. Bates, *Blossoming World*, p. 28. All future references to this work appear in the text.
2. Bates, *Vanished World*, p. 152. All future references to this work appear in the text.
3. Review of *The Two Sisters*, by H. E. Bates, *Living Age* 330 (21 August 1926):431.
4. H. E. Bates, *The Two Sisters* (London, 1926), p. 130. All future references to this work appear in the text.
5. Review of *The Two Sisters*, by H. E. Bates, *Nation and Atheneum* 39 (24 July 1926):476.
6. Bates, "Thomas Hardy and Joseph Conrad," p. 235. All future references to this work appear in the text.
7. Rayner Heppenstall, "New Novels," review of *The Cruise of the Breadwinner*, by H. E. Bates, *New Statesman and Nation* 32 (20 July 1946):53.
8. One play—*The Last Bread* (London, 1926)—preceded *The Two Sisters* into publication.
9. H. E. Bates, *The Modern Short Story: A Critical Survey* (London, 1972), pp. 206–7. All future references to this work appear in the text.
10. "New Books and Reprints," review of *Day's End*, by H. E. Bates, *TLS*, 5 July 1928, part 2, p. 506.
11. "Fiction Shorts," review of *Day's End*, by H. E. Bates, *Nation* 127 (10 October 1928):377.
12. "The New Books," review of *Day's End*, by H. E. Bates, *Saturday Review of Literature* 5 (5 January 1929):575.
13. H. E. Bates, "The Baker's Wife," in *Day's End and Other Stories* (London, 1928), p. 74. All future references to this collection appear in the text.
14. "The New Books," p. 575.
15. See Bates, *Modern Short Story*, p. 75, for a discussion of his indebtedness to Maupassant.

16. H. E. Bates, ed., Introduction to *Six Stories* (London, 1965), p. x.

17. H. E. Bates, "The Writer Explains," *Country Tales: Collected Short Stories* (London, 1938), p. 8.

18. "Mr. Bates's Short Stories," review of *Seven Tales and Alexander*, by H. E. Bates, *New Statesman* 34 (28 December 1929):398.

19. H. E. Bates, "A Comic Actor," in *Seven Tales and Alexander* (New York, 1930), p. 131. All future references to this collection appear in the text.

20. Edward Garnett, Foreword, *The Hessian Prisoner*, by H. E. Bates (London, 1930), p.7.

21. H. E. Bates, *Catherine Foster* (London, 1929), p. 222. All future references to this work appear in the text.

22. H. E. Bates, *Charlotte's Row* (London, 1931), p. 13. All future references to this work appear in the text.

Chapter Three

1. Bates, "The Writer Explains," p. 8.

2. H. E. Bates, "Charlotte Esmond," in *The Black Boxer: Tales* (London, 1932), p. 82. All future references to this collection appear in the text.

3. Graham Greene, "Short Stories," review of *The Woman Who Had Imagination and Other Stories*, by H. E. Bates, *Spectator* 152 (16 March 1934):424.

4. H. E. Bates, "The Story Without an End," in *The Woman Who Had Imagination and Other Stories* (London, 1934), p. 23. All future references to this collection appear in the text.

5. H. E. Bates, "The Station," in *Cut and Come Again: Stories*, Evensford ed. (London: Jonathan Cape, 1947), p. 115. All future references to this work appear in the text.

6. H. E. Bates, "Something Short and Sweet," in *Something Short and Sweet: Stories* (London, 1937), p. 54. All future references to this collection appear in the text.

7. H. E. Bates, *The Fallow Land* (London, 1932), p. 23. All future references to this work appear in the text.

8. H. E. Bates, *The Poacher* (London, 1935), p. 155. All future references to this work appear in the text.

9. H. E. Bates, *A House of Women*, Evensford ed. (London: Jonathan Cape, 1951), p. 11.

10. Bates, *Blossoming World*, p. 125. All future references to this work appear in the text.

11. H. E. Bates, *Spella Ho* (London, 1938), p. 11. All future references to this work appear in the text.

12. Bates, "Thomas Hardy and Joseph Conrad," p. 231.

Chapter Four

1. Half of the stories found in *My Uncle Silas: Stories* appeared in various earlier collections.

2. H. E. Bates, Pref., *My Uncle Silas: Stories* (London, 1939), p. 10. All future references to this collection appear in the text.

3. Mark Twain, "How to Tell a Story," in *The American Tradition in Literature*, ed. Sculley Bradley, Richard Beatty, E. Hudson Long, and George Perkins, 4th ed., 2 vols. (New York: Grosset and Dunlap, 1974), 2:181.

4. Bates, *Blossoming World*, p. 149. All future references to this work appear in the text.

5. H. E. Bates, "Fuchsia," in *The Beauty of the Dead and Other Stories* (London, 1940), p. 59. All future references to this collection appear in the text.

6. See H. E. Bates, *The World in Ripeness: An Autobiography* (Columbia, Mo., 1972), p. 33. All future references to this work appear in the text.

7. Fowler Hill, "France Underground," review of *Fair Stood the Wind for France*, by H. E. Bates, *New York Times*, 28 May 1944, p. 6.

8. Bates, *Vanished World*, p. 108.

9. H. E. Bates, *Fair Stood the Wind for France* (Boston, 1944), p. 116. All future references to this work appear in the text.

Chapter Five

1. See Chapter 8 for a brief discussion of the aesthetics of the novella.

2. H. E. Bates, Introduction to *Six Stories* (London: Oxford), p. xvii.

3. H. E. Bates, *The Cruise of the Breadwinner* (Boston, 1947), pp. 14–15. All future references to this work appear in the text.

4. Bates, *World in Ripeness*, p. 108. All future references to this work appear in the text.

5. H. E. Bates, *The Purple Plain* (Boston, 1947), p. 108. All future references to this work appear in the text.

6. H. E. Bates, *The Jacaranda Tree* (Boston, 1949), p. 24. All future references to this work appear in the text.

7. H. E. Bates, *The Scarlet Sword* (Boston, 1951), p. 23. All future references to this work appear in the text.

8. H. E. Bates, *Dear Life* (Boston, 1949), p. 13. All future references to this work appear in the text.

Chapter Six

1. Bates, "The Writer Explains," in *Country Tales*, p. 8.

2. H. E. Bates, "A Girl Called Peter," in *Colonel Julian and Other Stories* (Boston, 1952), p. 166. All future references to this collection appear in the text.

3. Bates, *World in Ripeness*, p. 87.

4. H. E. Bates, "The Maker of Coffins," in *The Daffodil Sky* (Boston, 1956), p. 118. All future references to this collection appear in the text.

5. H. E. Bates, "Queenie White," in *Sugar for the Horse* (London, 1957), p. 30. All future references to this collection appear in the text.

6. H. E. Bates, "The Cowslip Field," in *The Watercress Girl and Other Stories* (Boston, 1960), p. 9. All future references to this collection appear in the text.

7. H. E. Bates, "Lost Ball," in *The Enchantress and Other Stories* (Boston and Toronto, 1961), p. 47. All future references to this collection appear in the text.

8. H. E. Bates, "The Sun of December," in *The Wedding Party* (London, 1965), p. 102. All future references to this collection appear in the text.

Chapter Seven

1. See Bates, *Vanished World*, p. 157. All future references to this work appear in the text.

2. H. E. Bates, *Love for Lydia* (Boston, 1953), p. 38. All future references to this book appear in the text.

3. For a discussion of the autobiographical elements in *Love for Lydia*, see Bates, *World in Ripeness*, pp. 116–18. All future references to this work appear in the text.

4. H. E. Bates, *The Feast of July* (Boston, 1954), p. 3. All future references to this work appear in the text.

5. H. E. Bates, *A Breath of French Air* (Boston, 1959), p. 98.

6. H. E. Bates, *A Little of What You Fancy* (Boston, 1970), p. 210. All future references to this work appear in the text.

7. H. E. Bates, *The Darling Buds of May* (Boston, 1958), p. 7.

8. H. E. Bates, *Oh! to Be in England* (New York, 1964), p. 97.

9. H. E. Bates, *Hark, Hark, the Lark!* (Boston, 1961), p. 146.

10. H. E. Bates, *A Crown of Wild Myrtle* (New York, 1963), p. 72. All future references to this work appear in the text.

11. H. E. Bates, *A Moment in Time* (New York, 1964), p. 17. All future references to this work appear in the text.

12. H. E. Bates, *The Distant Horns of Summer* (London, 1967), p. 48. All future references to this work appear in the text.

Chapter Eight

1. Bates, Introduction to *Six Stories*, p. viii.

2. "Domestic Drama," review of *The Nature of Love*, by H. E. Bates, *TLS*, 18 September 1953, p. 593.

3. H. E. Bates, "The Grass God," in *The Nature of Love: Three Short Novels* (London, 1953), p. 163. All future references to this collection appear in the text.

4. H. E. Bates, "Night Run to the West," in *Summer in Salandar* (Boston and Toronto, 1957), p. 82. All future references to this collection appear in the text.

5. H. E. Bates, "An Aspidistra in Babylon," in *The Grapes of Paradise: Four Short Novels* (Boston and Toronto, 1960), p. 28. All future references to this collection appear in the text.

6. H. E. Bates, "The Golden Oriole," in *The Golden Oriole: Five Novellas*

(Boston, 1962), p. 109. All future references to this collection appear in the text.

7. H. E. Bates, "The Four Beauties," in *The Four Beauties* (London, 1968), p. 42. All future references to this collection appear in the text.

8. Bates, *World in Ripeness*, pp. 113−14.

9. H. E. Bates, *The Triple Echo* (London, 1970), p. 7. All future references to this work appear in the text.

Selected Bibliography

PRIMARY SOURCES

1. Short Fiction

An Aspidistra in Babylon: Four Novellas. London: Michael Joseph, 1960; as *The Grapes of Paradise: Four Short Novels*. Boston: Little, Brown and Co., 1960.

The Beauty of the Dead and Other Stories. London: Jonathan Cape, 1940.

The Black Boxer: Tales. London: Jonathan Cape, 1932; New York: R. Ballou, 1933.

The Bride Comes to Evensford. London: Jonathan Cape, 1943.

Colonel Julian and Other Stories. London: Michael Joseph, 1951; Boston: Little, Brown and Co., 1952.

Country Tales: Collected Short Stories. London: Readers' Union, 1938.

The Cruise of the Breadwinner. London: Michael Joseph, 1946; Boston: Little, Brown and Co., 1947.

Cut and Come Again: Fourteen Stories. London: Jonathan Cape, 1935.

The Daffodil Sky. London: Michael Joseph, 1955; Boston: Little, Brown and Co., 1956.

Day's End and Other Stories. London: Jonathan Cape; New York: The Viking Press, 1928.

Death of a Huntsman: Four Short Novels. London: Michael Joseph, 1957; as *Summer in Salandar*. Boston: Little, Brown and Co., 1957.

The Duet. London: Grayson and Grayson, 1935.

The Fabulous Mrs. V. London: Michael Joseph, 1964.

The Flying Goat. London: Jonathan Cape, 1939.

The Four Beauties. London: Michael Joseph, 1968.

A German Idyll. London: Golden Cockerel Press, 1932.

The Golden Oriole: Five Novellas. London: Michael Joseph; Boston: Little, Brown and Co., 1962.

The Good Corn and Other Stories. Edited by Geoffrey Halson. London: Longman, 1974.

The Greatest People in the World and Other Stories, by Flying Officer 'X.' London: Jonathan Cape, 1942; as *There's Something in the Air*. New York: A. Knopf, 1942.

H. E. Bates. Edited by Alan C. Cattel. London: Harrap, 1975.

The Hessian Prisoner. London: William Jackson, 1930.

The House With the Apricot and Two Other Tales. London: Golden Cockerel Press, 1933.

How Sleep the Brave and Other Stories, by Flying Officer "X." London: Jonathan Cape, 1943.

I Am Not Myself. London: Corvinus Press, 1939.

Mrs. Esmond's Life. London: E. Lahr, 1931.

My Uncle Silas: Stories. London: Jonathan Cape, 1939.

The Nature of Love: Three Short Novels. London: Michael Joseph, 1953; Boston: Little, Brown, and Co., 1954.

Now Sleeps the Crimson Petal and Other Stories. London: Michael Joseph, 1961; as *The Enchantress and Other Stories.* Boston: Little, Brown, and Co., 1961.

The Poison Ladies and Other Stories. Exeter: A. Wheaton and Co., 1976.

Sally Go Round the Moon. London: White Owl Press, 1932.

Selected Stories. London and Baltimore: Penguin Books, 1957.

Seven by Five: Stories 1926−61. London: Michael Joseph, 1963; as *The Best of H. E. Bates.* Boston: Little, Brown, and Co., 1963.

Seven Tales and Alexander. London: Scholartis Press, 1929. New York: The Viking Press, 1930.

Something Short and Sweet: Stories. London: Jonathan Cape, 1937.

The Spring Song and In View of the Fact That. London: E. Archer, 1927.

The Stories of Flying Officer "X." London: Jonathan Cape, 1952. Combines *The Greatest People in the World* and *How Sleep the Brave.*

The Story Without an End and the Country Doctor. London: White Owl Press, 1932.

Sugar for the Horse. London: Michael Joseph, 1957.

Thirty-One Selected Tales. London: Jonathan Cape, 1947.

Thirty Tales. London: Jonathan Cape, 1934.

A Threshing Day. London: M. and G. Foyle, 1931.

The Tree. London: E. Lahr, 1930.

The Triple Echo. London: Michael Joseph, 1970.

Twenty Tales. London: Jonathan Cape, 1951.

The Watercress Girl and Other Stories. London: Michael Joseph, 1959; Boston: Little, Brown, and Co., 1960.

The Wedding Party. London: Michael Joseph, 1965.

The Wild Cherry Tree. London: Michael Joseph, 1968.

The Woman Who Had Imagination and Other Stories. London: Jonathan Cape; New York: Macmillan Co., 1934.

2. Novels

A Breath of French Air. London: Michael Joseph; Boston: Little, Brown, and Co., 1959.

Catherine Foster. London: Jonathan Cape; New York: Viking Press, 1929.

Charlotte's Row. London: Jonathan Cape, 1931; New York: R. O. Ballou, 1932.

A Crown of Wild Myrtle. London: Michael Joseph, 1956; New York: Farrar, Straus, 1963.

The Darling Buds of May. London: Michael Joseph; Boston: Little, Brown, and Co., 1958.

Dear Life. Boston: Little, Brown, and Co., 1949; London: Michael Joseph, 1950.

The Distant Horns of Summer. London: Michael Joseph, 1967.

Fair Stood the Wind for France. London: Michael Joseph; Boston: Little, Brown, and Co., 1944.

The Fallow Land. London: Jonathan Cape, 1932; New York: R. O. Ballou, 1933.

The Feast of July. London: Michael Joseph; Boston: Little, Brown, and Co., 1954.

A House of Women. London: Jonathan Cape; New York: H. Holt, 1936.

The Jacaranda Tree. London: Michael Joseph; Boston: Little, Brown, and Co., 1949.

A Little of What You Fancy. London: Michael Joseph, 1970.

Love for Lydia. London: Michael Joseph, 1952; Boston: Little, Brown, and Co., 1953.

A Moment in Time. London: Michael Joseph; New York: Farrar, Straus, 1964.

Oh! to Be in England. London: Michael Joseph, 1963; New York: Farrar, Straus, 1964.

The Poacher. London: Jonathan Cape; New York: Macmillan Co., 1935.

The Purple Plain. London: Michael Joseph; Boston: Little, Brown, and Co., 1947.

The Scarlet Sword. London: Michael Joseph, 1950; Boston: Little, Brown, and Co., 1951.

The Sleepless Moon. London: Michael Joseph; Boston: Little, Brown, and Co., 1956.

Spella Ho. London: Jonathan Cape; Boston: Little, Brown, and Co., 1938.

The Two Sisters. London: Jonathan Cape; New York: Viking Press, 1926.

When the Green Woods Laugh. London: Michael Joseph, 1960; as *Hark, Hark, the Lark!* Boston: Little, Brown, and Co., 1961.

3. Other

Achilles and Diana, with Carol Baker. London: Dobson; New York: F. Watts, 1963. Juvenile.

Achilles and the Donkey, with Carol Baker. London: Dobson; New York: F. Watts, 1963. Juvenile.

Achilles and the Twins, with Carol Baker. London: Dobson; New York: F. Watts, 1965. Juvenile.

The Blossoming World: An Autobiography. London: Michael Joseph; Columbia: University of Missouri Press, 1971.

The Country Heart. London: Michael Joseph, 1949. Includes *In the Heart of the Country* and *O! More Than Happy Countryman.*

Country Life. London: Penguin Books, 1943.

The Country of White Clover. London: Michael Joseph, 1952.

The Day of Glory. London: Michael Joseph, 1945. Play.

The Day of the Tortoise. London: Michael Joseph, 1961.

Down the River. London: U. Gollancz; New York: H. Holt, 1937.
Edward Garnett. London: Parrish; Folcroft, Pa.: Folcroft Library Editions, 1950.
The Face of England. London: Batsford, 1952.
Flowers and Faces. London: Golden Cockerel Press, 1935.
Foreword. *A Terrible Day*, by David Garnett. London: William Jackson, 1932.
Holly and Sallow. Blue Moon Poem for Christmas, 1931. Broadside.
In the Heart of the Country. London: Country Life, 1942.
Introduction to *Six Stories.* Edited by H. E. Bates. London: Oxford University Press, 1965.
The Last Bread. London: The Labour Publishing Co., 1926. (play)
A Love of Flowers. London: Michael Joseph, 1971.
The Modern Short Story: A Critical Survey. London: T. Nelson and Sons, 1941; Boston: The Writer, 1941; The 1972 edition—Michael Joseph, London—contains a new preface by Bates.
O! More Than Happy Countryman. London: Country Life, 1943.
Pastoral on Paper. Newhythem, Eng.: Medway Corrugated Paper Co., n.d.
The Seasons and the Gardener: A Book for Children. Cambridge: At the University Press, 1940.
The Seekers. London: John and Edward Bumpus, 1926. Juvenile.
Song for December. (London?): n.p., 1928.
The Song of the Wren. London: Michael Joseph, 1972.
"Thomas Hardy and Joseph Conrad." In *The English Novelists: A Survey of the Novel by Twenty Contemporary Novelists.* Edited by Derek Verschoyle. London: Chatto and Windus, 1936, pp. 229–44.
Through the Woods: The English Woodland—April to April. London: U. Gallancz; New York: Macmillan Co., 1936.
The Tinkers of Elstow. London: Bemtose, n.d.
The Vanished World: An Autobiography. London: Michael Joseph; Columbia: University of Missouri Press, 1969.
The White Admiral. London: Dobson, 1968. Juvenile.
The World in Ripeness: An Autobiography. London: Michael Joseph; Columbia: University of Missouri Press, 1972.

SECONDARY SOURCES

1. Books and Parts of Books
Beachcroft, T. O. *The Modest Art: A Survey of the Short Story in English.* London: Oxford University Press, pp. 1, 57, 103, 114, 177, 185–86, 187, 188, 190, 212, 215. A brief discussion centering on Bates's use of Midland characters and themes.
Foster, John L. Introduction to *The Poison Ladies and Other Stories,* by H. E. Bates. Exeter: A. Wheaton and Co., 1976, pp. vii–viii. An overview composed primarily of quotations from Bates.

Frierson, William. *The English Novel in Transition, 1885—1940.* New York: Cooper Square Publishers, 1965, pp. 283, 306—8, 320, 321. Reflecting the influences of Hardy, Lawrence, and Chekhov, Bates's artistic detachment comes from his fundamental pessimism.

Garnett, David. Introduction to *Thirty Tales*, by H. E. Bates. London: Jonathan Cape, 1940, pp. 5—8. Holds Bates's work in high regard, but, "His one serious fault is that he is not as sensitive to words as he might be. . . . "

Garnett, Edward. Foreword to *The Hessian Prisoner*, by H. E. Bates. London: William Jackson, 1930, pp. 7—10. An overview of Bates's short fiction to date. Claims that "Alexander" is Bates's "high-water mark."

Miller, Henry. Preface to *The Best of H. E. Bates*. Boston: Little, Brown, and Co., 1963. Comments on Bates's skillful use of nature and his treatment of women, plus his humor and "obsession with pain." Concludes that the novella is best suited to his talents.

Peden, William. Foreword to the American Edition of *The Vanished World: An Autobiography*, by H. E. Bates. Columbia: University of Missouri Press, 1969. Contends that Bates has been undervalued in America and concludes that his treatment of nature is most memorable.

2. Articles

Alter, Robert. "New Fiction." Review of *The Best of H. E. Bates*. *New York Herald Tribune*, 29 September 1963, p. 18. Cites Bates's "unusual ability to enter into the world of the mute and incomprehending," plus his sensitivity to the power of sex.

Cosman, May. "Fun in France." Review of *A Breath of French Air*. By H. E. Bates. *Commonweal* 71 (4 December 1959):302—4. Sees Bates as moving toward "straight satire" with the Larkins as not merely the vehicle but the subject.

————. "Rabelais Adopted to English Propriety." Review of *The Darling Buds of May*. By H. E. Bates. *Commonweal* 68 (4 July 1958):356—57. Beneath the surface humor the novel has a serious side: Bates's answer to the "Angry Young Men."

Curtis, Dunham. "Reigning Duet." Review of *Colonel Julian*. By H. E. Bates. *Saturday Review*, 24 May 1952, p. 23. Bemoans supposition that Bates's reputation in America rests on novels of sex and violence rather than the finer short stories.

Davenport, Basil. "Stories Without Plot." Review of *Seven Tales and Alexander*. By H. E. Bates. *Saturday Review of Literature*, 8 November 1930, p. 305. Compares Bates's method to Katherine Mansfield's.

"Epics in Miniature." Review of *The Best of H. E. Bates*. *Times Literary Supplement*, 13 September 1963, p. 688. A fine overview of Bates's career, citing his pictorial style and cinematic techniques.

Greene, Graham. "Short Stories." Review of *The Woman Who Had Imagination*. By H. E. Bates. *Spectator*, 16 March 1934, p. 424. Fine discussion of Bates's indebtedness to Chekhov.

Hall, Hope. "Child's-eye View." Review of *The Watercress Girl*. By H. E. Bates. *Saturday Review*, 16 January 1960, p. 65. Discusses the sense of foreboding beneath the child's view.

Jenkins, Elizabeth. "New Fiction." Review of *Colonel Julian*. By H. E. Bates. *Manchester Guardian*, 29 June 1951, p. 4. The stories have "that classic quality of representing in one completely natural and realistic figure a whole scene or system of social life."

Mandel, Siegfried. "Schizophrenic Adventures." Review of *Dear Life*. By H. E. Bates. *Saturday Review of Literature*, 19 November 1949, p. 19. Bates's attempt to make the "real unreal" is like Poe, Strindberg, Kafka, and others.

Moon, Eric. "A Few Moments of Infinity." Review of *A Moment in Time*. By H. E. Bates. *Saturday Review*, 8 August 1964, p. 35. Bates has fallen far. The novel is merely sentimental.

Mortimer, Raymond. "Reviews: New Novels." Review of *Day's End*. By H. E. Bates. *Nation and Atheneum*, 9 June 1928, p. 332. One of the best reviews of this collection. Discusses characterization and use of nature.

Murry, Colin. "Without His Tutor." Review of *The Golden Oriole*. By H. E. Bates. *Time and Tide*, 19 May 1962, p. 34. Provocative review. Claims that Bates's fluency was his great strength and weakness. Edward Garnett, of Jonathan Cape, kept his excesses in check, but with Garnett's death in 1937, Bates's work begins to suffer.

Price, R. G. G. "New Fiction." Review of *An Aspidistra in Babylon*. By H. E. Bates. *Punch*, 10 February 1960, p. 239. Compares Bates to Maugham.

Romilly, Giles. "New Novels." Review of *The Nature of Love*. By H. E. Bates. *New Statesman and Nation*, 12 September 1953, p. 294. Compares Bates to Maugham and discusses the cinematic elements in the stories.

Stern, James. "Haunted Melford the Huntsman." Review of *The Sleepless Moon*. By H. E. Bates. *New York Times Book Review*, 22 April 1956, p. 4. Describes novel as a "beautifully written tragedy."

3. Dissertation

Vannatta, Dennis. "An Introduction to the Short Fiction of H. E. Bates." University of Missouri, 1978.

Index